Right Here, Right Now

Right Here, Right Now:

Seeing Your True Nature as Present Awareness

John Wheeler

NON-DUALITY PRESS

NON-DUALITY PRESS
6 Folkestone Road Salisbury SP2 8JP United Kingdom
www.non-dualitybooks.com

Cover artwork: John Gustard

First Printing: March 2006

ISBN 978-0-9551762-3-4

Preface

Is it possible to clearly point to something that cannot be seen? From John Wheeler comes the remarkable gift of beating the same drum at the same tempo with a fresh look at every concern. From the first word, it is clear that the author is speaking from direct honest experience and with the pure intent of bringing the reader to resolution. Because of this, the reader quickly gains confidence that the uncompromising message delivered in these pages is not just the opinion, concept, or belief of the author.

The drum that John beats so well is conveying the message that what you seek you already are. You will find many of your own questions in this book followed by answers that effortlessly remove the misconceptions that have been carried, perhaps for a lifetime. In coming to see what the author is pointing to, further questions and doubts will dissolve into the natural state of peace and completeness that is beyond words.

In a world where it appears that there is a you and a me, it is with lasting gratitude and without reservation that I say with absolute finality, that in the straightforward answers of this book is the key to end your search.

John Greven
Enid, Oklahoma
February, 2006

Table of Contents

1

Let the Mind Be

Question: Things are unfolding nicely here …

John: What is knowing that? In what is it all unfolding? Come back to that. Unfolding is in time. Reality is ever-present and timeless. Hone in on the core of timeless presence-awareness. Everything else comes and goes. This does not.

Q: It is relatively effortless.

John: Awareness is one hundred percent natural and effortless. When, in your experience, is it not shining? The fact of being present and aware is totally effortless. That is what you are, and it is already present. We overlooked it because we were looking for something exotic, but it has been right here all along!

Q: I recall reading about the mind dropping into an open state. Right now, the mind is very active, and it seems as though it still believes it is running the show.

John: You are still giving a bit of emphasis to the mind. The answer is not there! Let it be as it will. Are you controlling it? Do you have any power over it? No! Let it go. The golden gate of freedom lies in another direction. That in you which is present and aware is always free of the mind, just like the sun shining above the clouds. The sun never worries about clouds. Awareness is never bothered by thoughts. It is only interest in thoughts that binds us to them. There is no freedom or happiness available through looking to the mind.

The direct recognition of light and love is in the non-conceptual, non-mental apprehension of awareness. Thoughts form no barrier to this. Thoughts cannot be there without awareness, can they? So awareness is here. It is also presence, openness and love. Just turn to that. It is right there, always in you.

Q: There is a real desire here for it to settle down.

John: This will hang you up. It is a concept and puts the mind in conflict with itself. It is a sign that we are still looking to the mind for what is real. We put that expectation on the mind and it cannot deliver. What does love have to do with the mind? Let the mind be. It can be there or do anything. That is not a problem. Keep looking at that which is present and clear, not back at the mind. Do not renounce it, judge it or do anything with it. It is just a few passing clouds floating across a clear blue sky. What is seeing them? Who are you in relation to those thoughts?

Q: Is that openness something that will eventually occur?

John: No, because it is already present. We are just overlooking it. See if you can find the already present spaciousness in you.

Q: I suppose that is just another pointer, and I do not need to expect any further developments?

John: Drop the expectation of anything special happening in the future. That will keep you on the wheel. Your true nature is always in the present.

Q: I know what I am, but there is still a lot of wanting things to be a certain way. I think I still have some sense of being an individual. Do you have any suggestions for clearing this up? I think I have been over it every which way.

John: It is just some residual habits. They will take care of themselves as you settle in with the recognition of your true nature. There may still be a few concepts floating around like old cobwebs, just some subtle beliefs in the future, some residual tendency to look to the mind for a state that you do not have. You will eventually come to see those are false concepts, and then they will not trouble you any longer.

2

Just Keep It Simple

Q: I have been both fascinated and perplexed by non-duality for over a year now. I have tried to do the crucial self analysis of finding out who I am and where I exist. I realize that I am not my thoughts since I am still aware even when I have no thoughts. But I cannot say that I am not my body because my body is always here, it never disappears. Apparently, the conclusion I should have reached was that I am not the thoughts, I am not the body. Therefore, I am the underlying awareness. But I cannot arrive at this conclusion. What am I doing wrong? I hope you can help me.

John: Just keep it simple. Stop right now and notice the fact of your presence, which exists and is aware right now. Is there any difficulty in recognizing that fact? That is what you are. It is clear and present at all times and can never be doubted. Seeing this is not a conclusion of the mind. There is no need for a conclusion.

The recognition of the fact of presence-awareness is not done through the mind or the senses. When you ask yourself if you exist and if you are aware, the answer that comes is not a product of a chain of reasoning, but a direct, non-conceptual recognition. That is why they say 'non-conceptual awareness'. You cannot use the mind to recognize what is being pointed out. Yet it is easy to see, once you catch the pointer. The simplicity is the key.

You are present and aware. That is what you are. Everything else simply arises and sets in this presence, which is ever-present and clear as that knowingness that knows and, therefore, transcends all appearances. That is it in a nutshell.

Q: Thank you for your patient reply to my question. John, does it matter that much what my motivation is for wanting to awaken? My feeling is that I am partly motivated by the wish to truly know myself, but also partly motivated by my ego, which desires to be superior to ordinary, unawak-ened people.

John: Basically, everyone wants to be free and be happy. Everyone wants to know what is real. There is no need to second guess your motivation. This is just the mind coming in to evaluate things. Just follow your heart. The focus naturally falls off of the mind and its worries and concerns. What is coming up is just a little residue of the past conditioning. There is no harm. There is no need to worry too much about it. The ideas of 'superior' and 'ordinary' people are just some old concepts. You exist and are aware right now. It has nothing to do with superior or ordinary. It is a simple fact and transcends all such mental labels and categories.

Q: I go through periods (sometimes minutes, sometimes hours) of feeling a deep stillness and peace, and then I am straight back into strong thoughts and feelings about my life situation, all the bad things that have happened in my life and all the people that have wronged me. Do these strong thoughts and feelings slowly subside as one rests more and more in awareness? It is a bit of a roller coaster ride.

John: Yes. The focus on thoughts subsides. Continue to notice the fact of being or presence-awareness—whatever you want to call it. Thoughts come and go but you remain—clear, present and solid as a rock. We pay attention to thoughts because we think they say something about who we are, but they do not. We have been looking in the wrong direction. Once this confusion is cleared up the focus returns to what we really are.

Q: Is it really true that there is nothing I can do to awaken, because there is no 'I' there? If this is so, then is the process of awakening simply your awareness triggering a resonance in my awareness? I feel as if I am running around like a headless chicken seeking that which I can never find.

John: No. I do not agree that there is nothing you can do. Just investigate what you are. Have a look to verify the pointers. If there is nothing you can do, there is no use talking about this. The investigation does reveal that what we took ourselves to be is not true. It also clarifies what we are. In the light of clear seeing, the separate doer is seen to be false. But you need to look and see this for yourself. It sounds like a paradox, but it really is not. We just clear up the doubts and come back to a recognition of what is true. Nothing is really changed but the confusion is removed.

Q: Sorry for these questions. I know that I could probably ask you questions for the next decade and it probably would not get me any closer to what I seek, because ultimately there is no magic formula for awakening.

John: Do not hold too tightly to the concept of awakening. It is tantalizing, but it is still only a concept. Whatever you are, you are even now. It is just seeing what is present. There is no need for awakening or any event or attainment. That is a concept which keeps you looking in the wrong direction.

3

We Must Look for Ourselves

Question: Your response to my last email about not expecting fireworks clarified things wonderfully. All that is left now is just looking, a relaxing back into this awareness that contains everything, a process of allowing this simple, absolutely constant, unchanging and utterly simple feeling of being to become foreground, while allowing the contents of awareness to come and go. It can be done at any time, while at work or play, while walking along a street or sitting with a cup of coffee, while talking with a friend. No lotus postures are needed, no quiet place, no special practice.

Now I know, really know, what you and others have been saying about thoughts and concepts and about authority. There can be no authority when it comes to this. There is no teaching we can accept unchecked and untested. We must look for ourselves, see by direct looking to find out whether or not what you or any other teacher has been saying is true or not. And that looking cannot be with the mind, since the mind cannot know this.

During my first meeting with Bob Adamson, I mentioned that, when reading Krishnamurti many years ago, I experienced what can only be described as a wall, as concept after concept, belief after belief, was torn down until there was nowhere left to look. I experienced it again during the meeting with Bob as a sense of frustration, an exasperation that I now recognize as the mind banging into the limits of what it can know. How obvious it turned out to be once it was pointed out, a simple 180-degree turn of attention inward to what is doing the looking.

John: Nice to hear from you. All this is resonating wonderfully for you and the seeing is clear. You met Bob Adamson, so there is precious little I can add! I like your statements about authority. No authority, teacher or sage can give us what we already are. Still the simple pointing back to the ever-present is greatly appreciated! You are doing a pretty good job of it yourself!

4

Shining in Plain View

Question: I would like to share some thoughts and perhaps hear your input. Many moments when suffering is observed there is a recognition of its illusoriness. So there are no questions. It seems like you have said all that can be said about who I am. Not only that, but the direct experience has occurred. So, the pendulum of experience goes on and 'I' do not care for it so much anymore. I suffer the bad moments and enjoy the good ones. And I keep asking who is there to suffer or enjoy.

Some cul-de-sac concepts keep popping up though. One of them is that the experience of seeing my true nature, a month ago, was very intense and emotionally charged. It was like I was a shining star in an infinite, loving and tranquil heart, accompanied by the clear view of the absence of 'me'. Now, there is no such experience in this moment. And there is a seeking of that experience, which traps the mind into seeking an imaginary moment based on memory. It feels like a 'catch 22', like I will be happy only if those experiences occur. At the same time, when my true nature of happiness or awareness reveals itself, even for a split second, the feeling of love and certainty is there.

Another concern is about the times when the mind is either engrossed in some activity, like playing the cello, tennis or at the computer, or else completely lost in some pleasant or unpleasant imaginary sequence of events. There is no possibility of self-inquiry at those times. It seems obvious that nothing can be done about that, but the frustration arising from perceiving such an amount of 'lost time' keeps recurring. I cannot quite pinpoint the relation of these experiences to the belief of being a separate entity.

Apart from that, at times there is a fluidity, effortlessness and formlessness to life which is new. And freedom and gratitude seem to breeze in and out effortlessly. The thought and feeling often arises, 'Look, all is quiet and perfect! Where are you and all the suffering?'

John: Continue to come back to the recognition of your true nature. It is not an experience or moment of clarity that comes and goes. We are looking for something constant and always available. It does not depend on moments of seeing or things dropping away. For even through those changing states, you cannot deny your presence, which exists and is aware. Coming back to that, you settle down with the understanding that there is something clear, bright and steady right within you at all times. Can you truly say that what you are comes and goes or is not present now or at any moment?

That flower is constant and ever-present in the heart. It is truly what you are. There may appear to be a wavering between recognizing that clear presence and the residual interest or belief in the self-centered thoughts and feelings due to old habits of the mind. This gives the appearance that the clarity is coming and going. It is something of an illusion, like feeling that the train is motionless and the world outside is moving. When you explore it a bit, you see this is not really true.

Suffering and doubts are only thoughts. The simplicity of this is breathtaking and its implications are immense. Those thoughts generally revolve around some view or notion of ourselves as being limited and apart from the deeper truth. But is it really true? Are we really apart from what is being pointed out as the reality? Looking a bit into this question with curiosity and interest exposes the beliefs and continues to lay bare the immediate availability of clarity.

These are just some reflections that came up to share, based on my experience. I had the exact same experience that you are sharing, so I know it is possible to resolve these doubts.

Q: Thank you for your message. It is so beautiful how deeply and clearly your words ring. If I may, I would like to discuss these and other issues more, even though all these questions do not feel really serious anymore, in a way. There is an underlying understanding that it is all conceptual. It is like everything is a passing movie, including the senses and the world which the mind creates from their input. Nevertheless, it feels good and right to somehow neutralize the questions and doubts by seeing them against the mirror of your responses. There is gratitude for being able to do this at this time.

John: Have no doubt. All of this is settling in quite well. It is like a flower—it just unfolds and reveals itself. Once you get a clear pointing to the heart of the matter and there is a resonance with it, the rest just blossoms. You see more and more clearly the simplicity of what is present and (as is happening) the conceptual ideas that we used to take for granted start to stand out as artificial and unnecessary. Talking about this is good. It is just a temporary reminder until the understanding settles in. Then you need no pointers or guidance. What you are seeking to know is shining in plain view.

5

The Suffering of Others

Question: I feel stuck. I am concerned about the suffering of others. I have talked to some teachers about this and received some pointers, but they feel like temporary fixes. I do not seem to see past all of the suffering I perceive around me. Maybe it is just an appearance, but I do not seem to be able to divorce myself from the seeming reality of the appearance. I feel overwhelmed at times by what I experience personally within my own family. The suffering is unabated. I somehow thought that getting an understanding of my true nature would alleviate the suffering or put it in a different light in a way that I could understand it.

Even in the few days since we met my outlook on the world has changed. Yes, I do realize that the awareness has not changed. I do not know what more I need to understand, or how to apply it. I am not a dummy, and yet I do not seem to be catching on to what others have realized. What can I do about the suffering?

John: The urge to alleviate our own or others' suffering is a worthwhile effort, but we need to lay the groundwork first. To truly be free of suffering requires that we thoroughly understand it. Whatever we understand, we are free of. So, I would suggest looking deeply into suffering to understand what it is. Where does it come from? How is it created? How is it sustained? What is its relation to who we truly are? In seeing this clearly, the proper response will be clear.

One possible pitfall is trying to divorce oneself from the appearance. This is too much of a duality and is not natural. Another pitfall is believing that others have something we do not. This is not really true, but the concept generates mental doubt and additional suffering.

The motto seems to be 'Physician, heal thyself!' You must first find the freedom from suffering within yourself. This will have profound effects on your view about the suffering of others. It is not 'my' suffering and 'their' suffering. It is one movement, one mechanism at work, whether here or there. So make sure your understanding of suffering is clear. Then you will be in a much better position to respond to the perceived suffering of others.

6

Appearances Can Take Care of Themselves

Question: Recently a friend sent me your book *Awakening to the Natural State* and besides starting to read it, I also took a look at your web site. Four or five years of non-duality lectures and visiting some teachers put me on this road. Before that, I spent sixteen years studying the teachings of Gurdjieff and Ouspensky. I do admire your simplicity and how you go straight to the point.

I have an issue that has been occupying some psychological space these days. I am hoping to hear your view on this. I am a father of three children. I have to maintain two families, keep up with child support and so on. Reading your material I encountered something you wrote to one of your correspondents:

'Imagine your current life with all mental problems and confusing emotions removed'.

My observations prove me that my psycho-physical organism has been programmed since childhood with an exaggerated sense of responsibility from my parents. I would say it is almost within my muscles! And this of course provokes a lot of unnecessary thinking in relation to many functional tasks that I need to perform in order to keep the whole thing going, especially in these times of financial and health pressures. The understanding that all thoughts, emotions and feelings appear within and from the whole is deeply embedded after some years of reading about non-duality and meetings with various teachers. Still, the question remains—what is the role of the body or the body-mind organism, since all these tendencies were created since infancy and are part of the cellular tissue?

In your experience, does the understanding of who we are dissolve these cellular-muscular imprints that are part of our programming? Or is it more that the understanding shifts the sense of identity and these phenomena, while still occurring because of our programming, no longer feed the illusion of being separate and unique? Or is both? I am asking these questions because reading your (beautifully put) description of peace, there arose in me the sense that 'in the future'—if I am lucky and make efforts to 'be' the understanding—I will reach this state.

John: What you find is that with the dawning of the recognition of your nature as the already-free presence-awareness itself, there is little concern for the configuration of the content in the appearance (body, mind, conditioning and so on). The main thing is to know what you are. The appearances can take care of themselves quite nicely. The habit to reference the appearance and ask about what will happen in the future is still missing the ever-present and obvious fact of your innate present freedom. Your being is now. It is not a future event or realization. All looking to the future is a false concept. If you are waiting for the future to know who you are, you will wait forever.

Q: Thank you for your reply. There are still some questions unresolved, but I know, by their very nature, that they will not be resolved ever! Your words sound as if they are coming directly from the center of the understanding and that is what makes them powerful. For me, the understanding seems to be clouded by dark clouds and makes me feel as if I am living in two worlds at the same time, one pure and radiant and untouched and the other somber, grave and complex. Perhaps this is the nature of duality.

John: Just keep the focus on the bright and clear presence of your true nature. That is always available and right within as that simple sense of knowing, existence and peace. It is so clear and present that we overlook it. It is the light of awareness illuminating all thoughts, the existence supporting all appearances and the light of love and peace behind all feelings. That is you, even now. Have faith in that. That is what it comes down to. That is all that is being pointed to.

Q: Thank you again for these words that came just at the right time, when they were most needed.

7

The Cessation of Seeking

Question: I have left things to settle for a while. In the last contact, I asked about omnipresence. You responded with questions like, 'Does it have limits or location?' and so on. I think this and other difficulties came from old concepts and a long-term search for—and an expectation of—something exotic. Seeing that I am awareness brought the cessation of seeking. I had found what I was looking for (what was never lost but simply overlooked). What a relief! Then there was the realization that there is not and never has been an individual in here.

This all happened while reading your site several weeks ago. Some old tendencies continued for a while, but now I am pleased to say that it is clear that I am awareness (just as I saw), that all else is an appearance and that it is the nature of the human mind to look for patterns and tell stories. I see that all appears in awareness and that awareness is looking out through these eyes, too. I continue to read my favorite subject (non-duality) but without trying to gain something. It is great to finally read with understanding instead of confusion. There has, as you said, been an unfolding. After about a month, I looked back over my life and could see it as one long dream. That has now ended. Clarity is the great prize, if I can use such terminology.

Once more I would like to thank you for your part in this—even if you had no choice, as I do not in typing this!

John: I am glad to get your e-mail and hear how the recognition of what is clear and present in you has been recognized. The dream of separation ends with a little bit of looking to see if it ever occurred. As you find, it did not! That recognition pretty well winds up the show. I am happy to hear the good news.

8

There Is No Need for Awakening

Question: Thank you for your time and especially your message! Is the key just being here and being present? Or is it a knowing of something? These two seem very different. When present, there is existing in a state of 'not knowing'. But to just 'know' who you are beyond the mind seems to be a different experience and feeling than simply being present. Also does the whole deal come down to simply watching with awareness? One well-known teacher recommends that we be present as the watcher of what happens within and without. Can you please respond to these questions?

John: Are you present? Are you aware? Any doubts about this? Presence and awareness are really two words pointing to the same thing. Your presence is aware. Your awareness is present. It (you) is present and clear and utterly beyond doubt right now. That is it. That is what I am pointing to as your real nature. Seeing it, knowing it, or recognizing it is neither sudden nor gradual, because it is already present beyond doubt. Very simple!

Q: Oh! So there is no such thing as becoming present or aware? We are that.

John: Yes. You are already what you are.

Q: So what is the whole idea of the present moment?

John: It is just a concept without much real value.

Q: And then, since we are that, is it just a removing of the mind or thoughts that causes the awakening?

John: There is no need for awakening. That is also just a concept. What is the need for awakening when you are already present and aware? You are that.

Q: So it is just noticing that the mind covers it or gets in the way?

John: In a sense this is true. We are just not noticing what is real and instead we are focusing on imaginary thoughts. Yet the truth is always shining in plain view, even if there are thoughts!

Q: What causes all of the suffering?

John: See the article *The Antidote for Suffering** for my take on it.

Q: Is there such a thing as awakening then?

John: No! If there is awakening, it is just seeing that you do not need any such thing!

---

*Chapter 25. p.72

9

There Is No Need to Remember Yourself

Question: I know I am pure awareness mentally, and have known it throughout my whole being.

John: There is no need to label this as mental knowing. You are aware now, right? You know it. That is not a mental knowing. You are quite aware of your real being, even now, not as an intellectual matter. Have confidence in your direct experience.

Q: I thought I was home free after a particularly powerful experience of being pure awareness.

John: Awareness is not an experience. It is an ever-present fact as the background of all experiences. Looking for experiences clouds the simplicity of it. You do not become free, as you are not a bound entity who needs to get 'there'. You are awareness now. It is freedom itself. That is what you are. You do not need any experiences or events for this.

Q: I recently ended a relationship, and in the emotional turbulence I feel as if I lost my knowing.

John: Yes, but did you lose the fact of your presence and fact of awareness? So did you really lose what is being pointed to? Absolutely not! So just drop that belief and embrace your ever-present true nature which has not left you, even for an instant.

Q: Do you have any pointers for me to help me remember who I am at all times?

John: There is no need. Remembering is just a mental state. You are that which knows memory and non-memory. You illumine both. There is no need to remember yourself, because you are yourself. Just take note of this fact. Question and discard any beliefs that come up that say anything different. It just comes down to seeing the facts and letting go of any wrong beliefs.

10

Presence-Awareness Never Waivers

Question: Many thanks for your last email. Things are still adjusting and the process appears to be needing time.

John: Only see that what is being pointed out is completely present. If you see that life adjusts and unfolds right in the ever-clear and available presence-awareness that you are—then no harm! In truth, there is no time involved in any of this. Time itself is an idea appearing and disappearing right in awareness. That is fully clear and present at all times.

Q: One nice aspect about all this is the simple understanding that there are really no problems in life.

John: Very true! Good seeing.

Q: Any incident or arrangement of events might appear as a problem or in some way deserving of anger, disappointment and so on. But it seems that everything invariably works out absolutely perfectly, and so-called negative events are seen to be part of a necessary flow. Anyway, that's how it appears without labeling things, I guess.

John: This sounds very clear to me.

Q: The direct sense of myself as presence became less direct over the past couple of weeks, but at least the normal panic to re-find what I wrongly thought had been found in the first place did not occur.

John: Look head on at this and see if presence, being, awareness (whatever we call it) ever became less, diminished or departed. You will be amazed to see that it did not. That is the key to realizing that it actually never wavers. We thought it did, but we were not looking clearly. We just took the mind's assumption that it became less to be true.

Q: I looked at some of your newer articles yesterday and one phrase struck a chord: 'You are the principle of life'. This is a phrase that I have needed to hear somehow. The words are spot on as far as I am concerned. It is that truth that I have intuitively known—life needs me for it to be here. It is that simple, fundamental truth which comes to the fore and then retreats.

John: Well, keep this simple. In direct experience, does life itself ebb and flow? Perhaps it is the ever-present background that everything else rises and set upon—even the idea that it retreats.

Q: There are people who are starting, unconsciously to search for themselves, yet still suffering from the concurrent feeling of lack and dissatisfaction. Perhaps it is these people who might, to the outside world, appear most judgmental and generally negative. There are a few people in my life right now who I feel could be on the verge of breaking into all this, but somehow it is over the horizon for them. As a result, they appear locked in a cycle of disappointment and losing their sense of perspective.

My girlfriend is an example of this. Her dissatisfaction seems to me to be something actually quite close to breaking through to a realm where the sense that she needs to uncover her true identity might start to arise. It is a real mystery and one that I have less and less willingness to try to control and twist. But there really is a wonderful mystery or even magic to the way things evolve. It is just a kind of sense which cannot be proved or disproved in any way.

John: What I have learned is that people eventually come around in their own time. There is no forcing anyone to look for themselves. I like Bob Adamson's statement: 'Some appearances turn back and realize themselves, and some do not. But it does not matter because no one has ever left presence anyway'. This leaves things completely free with no demand or expectation about others.

Q: As the principle of life, it all happens despite me, and there is no moving nearer or further to anything.

John: Now that sounds spot on! Keep in touch.

11

Discard False Ideas

Question: I am trying to figure out what to do in order to realize the truth of my being. After going through the answers on your web site, I am still scratching my head. You say 'look and see' what is there and what is false. I think I am a bit mixed up because I have heard that attention is a function of the mind and cannot help us in seeing what is real. That seems correct, and yet, 'look and see' seems to mean 'pay attention to'. And this seems like not just the right thing, but the only thing, to do.

A friend of mine suggested that just relaxing with it is important. Relaxing is not even necessary with the 'presence' and 'awareness' part. But relaxation may be necessary to notice the joy. I become frustrated when I see all the letters on your site from correspondents who have seen the truth, for whom the 'I' has dropped, and who are just noticing the dust of old beliefs occasionally floating by. I would like to see it fully, as well as being it. Is there really nothing to get? Exactly what, if anything, is to be done?

John: The idea that we are not there and that there is some experience 'out there' that we need to get is itself the problem. It is totally false and can never be fulfilled—because it is not true. You cannot fulfill a false belief. Those ideas will keep troubling you until you question them. You do not need to know, get, attain or figure out the truth of who you are. You are already who you are. At this stage, it is only false ideas that are hanging you up. It is false ideas that cause anxiety, questions, doubts and suffering. These come in like a cloud obscuring the ever-present sun. Has the sun gone anywhere? No!

Your true nature is always present as being and awareness. That is peace and joy itself. When the attention focuses on false ideas based on a wrong view of what we are, it appears as if the ever-present joy is clouded over. That is all that is going on. Whenever that is not going on, life is pure innocence, joy and peace. See the simplicity of this. This recognition provides the solution to the end of suffering. Follow the mind's false ideas and there is the appearance of suffering. Be as you are and do not alight on the mind's self-centered beliefs and there is peace.

If you want something to do, recognize and discard false ideas. Do not give the mind's ideas and beliefs about what you are too much importance. You are not a limited being in need of something. All those ideas are a false. You are that principle of awareness right now, and you always have been. I will keep telling you this until the message strikes home. Then you will not need me or anyone because you will know it for yourself.

12

Finding Peace and Ending Suffering Is Possible

Question: I feel completely OK with what you say in your book and in your correspondence, but I find a contradiction which makes me a bit confused. You say that there is no separate entity, no doer, nothing to do and so on. But then you also say to look for the 'I', investigate false ideas for yourself, do your homework and so on. How do you explain this seeming contradiction? Is there something yet that this phantom 'I' has to do?

John: Just for the record, I do not say there is nothing to do. Otherwise, why talk about all this? To one who believes himself to be an individual, the suggestion is made to find that individual. It is an antidote given to a phantom that believes itself to be real. In looking, the natural intelligence discovers that there never has been a separate person. When you realize what your real nature is, no teachings or pointers are needed.

Basically, all words and pointers are self-contradictory. They are like a temporary medicine to cure an illness. So follow the pointers and see the fact of your own being that is ever-present and clear at all times. That is what all these words are pointing to. The pointers are not what is being pointed to.

If you have seen that there is no individual, then your seeking and questions, by definition, are done. And you do not need me or anyone else to confirm anything. At all times you shine as that principle of presence-awareness beyond thought. That is the essence. Everything else is just a pointer to assist you to notice this. Is there a 'you' to notice it? No! You are that, even now. That is the final pointer I can offer.

Q: So when you recommend to investigate for yourself, actually you do not speak to anybody? This is just a tool?

John: Yes, just a tool to resolve a question. Once the question is resolved, you do not hang onto the tool. It is useless in and of itself. It is just a temporary device.

Q: One well-known teacher often says that you are totally helpless.

John: I recommend that you realize what your true nature is and discover the cause of suffering. The other approach can lead to a 'defeatist' attitude for some people.

Q: He also suggests that we see how the mind is running the show. Would you say that this is similar to the seeing and investigating you talk about?

John: If you are suffering and want to know what is real, the way is open to seek out the time-tested pointers that work and apply them for yourself. Then your questions and doubts are resolved. Finding peace and ending suffering is possible. It just takes understanding of what is true about ourselves and what is the root cause of suffering. This can be seen and known. This leads to a life of freedom.

13

There Is No Awakened Person

Question: When this understanding settles in what happens? Life just goes on?

John: Just as before! But the root of suffering and doubt is removed. Still, all goes on quite well. Your experience of it is different because you are clear about your true nature.

Q: I do notice that when I am present or aware, I do not get caught up in all the normal B.S. of regular life or thinking.

John: Do not divide who you are from presence-awareness. It is not a state that comes and goes. There really is no 'I', as such. That is the basic illusion. You are awareness right now. There is no separate 'I' in the picture at all. If you think there is, try to find it. It is that belief alone, ultimately, that is driving the confusion and doubts.

Q: It seems that 'being here' makes all the difference (the difference between being conscious and unconscious).

John: You are always that and you are always here. Have a look and see if you can doubt awareness. And can you find yourself as something apart from that? That is the heart of the matter. Until this is clarified, the doubts go on. Once this is seen, there are no more doubts.

Q: Is there free will or choice?

John: Both are concepts. They both imply an entity who has or does not have free will. But is there an entity? I have never found one. If you look closely, thoughts, feelings and experiences emerge spontaneously and without reference to a person. The person is an assumption, but there is not one.

Q: It seems that there really is choice. I can say or do what I feel like doing right now.

John: Not really at all. Do you choose your thoughts? Really look into this. This is incredibly liberating.

Q: All of the stupid normal interaction between humans is so childish and meaningless. Is it correct to say that an 'awakened' person does not get caught up in all of that so frequently and consistently?

John: There is no awakened person. This is a total illusion. Your own present being is all that is to be known. All questions come from not being clear about this fundamental issue. If you want to be clear and direct, make this the key point of investigation.

14

Slogans Are Not Going to Help You

Question: I think I sense what you are pointing at when you say that life does not ebb and flow at all.

John: Everything ebbs and flows in the presence that you are.

Q: Perhaps what is forgotten is that life is a dream, which is meaningless and does not matter.

John: I do not quite see it like this. This is too much of a mental judgment. Life is what it is—a movement in awareness. No judgments apply, as they all come in from the mind based on words and conditioning. Why call life meaningful or meaningless—it just is. There can still be a tremendous amount of care and love, by the way. Compassion and love are also there in the presence-awareness that you are. Love is the ultimate value.

Q: As a child, there was a knowing of this. Behind everything there was a constant sense of flowing and fluidity and timelessness. Surely, becoming an adult just means taking things to be important and to matter.

John: Or just taking on board a large number of unverified concepts. People are old because they are full of unexamined and limited beliefs. Otherwise, that child-like innocence is right there, in spite of age.

Q: When one remembers one is dreaming, there is a deep intuitive knowing of the one who is outside the dream.

There is a very subtle distancing from things and a new love for everything.

John: True. It is the same with this waking state. You are always behind and beyond, even in the midst of it.

Q: Life is a dream right? It has come out of nowhere and is a changing set of appearances. Nothing matters right?

John: Like I said, this is a bit too mental. Things matter at the appropriate level of appearance. See the world as a passing appearance and give it the appropriate level of attention it needs. Your child may be a passing appearance subject to birth and death, but that does not mean that you do not love him, care for him and tend to him to the best of your ability.

Q: Even enlightenment and happiness do not matter, it seems.

John: Being happy and free, living without illusion—what else matters?

Q: I do not want to get carried away with another slogan and I am aware that the 'life is just a dream' slogan is all over the place in seekers' minds.

John: Life is dream is a superficial statement to me. People go around saying this but may not have a depth of self-knowledge or lasting experience of freedom. Realize your true nature and expose the core cause of suffering and doubts. Slogans are not going to help you do this.

Q: All I can say is that I do not want any slogans anymore, but I often think to myself, what is the final understanding, the understanding to die with?

John: Know your true nature. Every serious seeker who found some kind of lasting deep understanding, peace or freedom has, in the end, resolved this issue. Most people are living under a complete misunderstanding of themselves. This leads to tremendous ignorance and suffering. If you resolve this for yourself, then your life in the world will have a great value for yourself and others. Without this, life is as good as wandering in a dream. To me that would have no meaning or value.

15

You Are Already Free

Question: Darn it! It is really quite baffling that there can be this clear seeing that the 'I' is always and only a thought arising. One after another, 'I' this, 'me' that, until finally there is this absorption in it. How can that be seen (as I do!) and still the absorption and mesmerization in it does not seem to end? I know there is some momentum, but it would seem that once it is clearly seen that it would be over. At times there is just this understanding and letting things unfold. And then there is frustration, wrapped around the 'I' arising in thought.

John: Who wants the momentum to end? See that as just a subtle concept for some entity who wants to arrive somewhere.

You are, even now, fully present and aware. Have you found any reason to doubt that? Have you ever moved from that, in spite of whatever thoughts arise? You shine without wavering in and through all thoughts, feelings and perceptions. It is so elegant and simple, isn't it? You are not a separate person at all, but that open and ever-free light of presence-awareness. It is just a simple truth. Know this and be at peace. All the peace, clarity and joy is shining within as the presence-awareness that you are. No one can give this to you, and no one can take it away. It is what you are.

Just see thoughts for what they are: passing shadows, fleeting motes of dust dancing in the light of your own being. Even self-centered thoughts and 'I' thoughts are just thoughts. They cannot be there without your own presence, can they?

Remember, there is no becoming free. Nothing needs to drop. See what is real and true and the illusions just melt away.

You do not even care, because you are already free. A lifetime of ongoing 'I' thoughts still would not be a problem because the fact of your being is never even touched.

Worrying about thoughts is giving them too much reality. Waiting for something to be over is just a concept. Abandon it! Nothing needs to be over. Make sure to see that freedom is already present. Then look back at thoughts and see that they are false. Do not wait for thoughts to disappear. Just see them as being false and inapplicable. Then it does not matter if they leave or stay—you do not believe them anymore. This is the key, not whether they are there or not. If you get hung up on whether certain thoughts are present or not, you will be stuck because you are not controlling them anyway, are you? If you go that route, you box yourself in a corner.

Once their falseness is seen, they will go of their own accord, naturally. There will be no concern if they are present or not. The real freedom is when you see that you are free whether thoughts appear or not. Awareness remains the constant backdrop of all thoughts. That is utterly untouched by all the thoughts, concepts and emotions. That is what you are. You are already free.

Follow up ...

Q: I have read your note over several times. It is great. It is elegant and simple. Know this and be at peace. The 'know' part is there and not there. Sometimes I see it and it is clear. At other times it is like pulling teeth to see it.

John: What exactly is 'it' that you are seeing? And who is the 'I' that knows 'it' or not, sees 'it' or not? Is your true nature that which is present and aware in you, something that appears and disappears? The subtle idea that there is some understanding that comes and goes is a false idea. As long as that idea is believed in, we seem to overlook what is present.

Be very clear on what is being pointed out. It is the simple fact of your present nature and what that is. You find in the end that it is not about getting or losing it, seeing it or even noticing it. All those are just mental activities. By nature they come and go. Remember, the answer is not in the mind. By looking for some understanding or experience in the mind, we are looking in the wrong direction. Once you really see this, the focus goes off of the mind. The idea of getting something that you do not have is no longer believed. Believe me, everything the mind says about this spiritual stuff is pretty much false and useless.

If you think that you do not have 'it', you can do two things. Take the idea to be true and wait for 'it' to happen, which it never will. Why? Because it is a false concept. What is being pointed to is not a future event. Or else you can question the idea, see it as false and stop believing it. Where does that leave you? Right here and now in the presence-awareness that you are and have never left. Then you are not thinking about anything, just being yourself, the natural state.

It is not about understanding anything or getting anything, not even enlightenment, which is a total concept. Instead, it is about abandoning any remaining false ideas. Then the natural state stands naked and revealed. That is your own present nature.

Q: I suppose that all I can do is to just keep noticing.

John: Noticing or not noticing are just thoughts. What do they appear in? That is so fundamental that it does not even need to be noticed. It is. Who is the 'I' doing all this anyway? Are you some entity that must do something? The statement implies you are not yet 'there' and there is something to do or some event in the future to wait for. Question these beliefs. There is great freedom in abandoning false beliefs. Nothing is added, but useless static drops out of the picture.

Even the treasured spiritual concepts must be questioned. None of them are really true. The truth is the fact of your own being, even now. Turn away from the mind concepts, and everything is wide open, available, clear and resolved right now.

16

The Answer Is Not in Thought

Question: When the question arises 'Am I this mind and all its chatter?' or 'What was I before this mind began and what will I be when it stops?' then there is a shift. I am not this mind. Whether it says the universe is real or unreal, what does that really matter or mean? The truth is more real than anything the mind thinks is real. I see this now. What a 'bang!' when you notice you have been looking in completely the wrong direction! This truth has to be lived, not thought! When the mind steps off center-stage, finally things can be seen for how wonderful they are. Not wonderful as a judgment, but wonderful because there is nothing between them and me. Thanks for all your help and guidance.

John: This is striking home. Look away from the mind and you see that your being as presence-awareness is clear beyond any doubt at all. You can never doubt the fact of your own being. And this doubtless being, which is existent and aware, is all that is being pointed to. The answer is not in thought. You know thought. That in you which knows thought is what you actually are.

17

Keep It Simple and Look for Yourself

Question: My main problem is residual emotional turbulence from an ended relationship. It rises up and takes over my perception. I lose my peaceful feeling that normally is always present.

John: If you are shooting for a continuous feeling of emotional peace, you are going to be disappointed! Emotions are constantly changing and swirling through. See that your awareness or your being stays steady and constant right through them all. Lock your sights on the fact of being, rather than responding to the thoughts and feelings going through. Otherwise you are bobbing like a cork on the sea, tossed by each wave. This is not about getting the thoughts and feelings to line up, or even to be pleasant. They are what they are. And do we control them, anyway? As the recognition of your true nature settles in you will find that all the other issues sort themselves out naturally. Let the recognition return to what is always clear and present within. This does not depend on states or outer situations being a certain way.

Q: What is locking the sights? The mind? I know we are awareness, but how can we observe ourselves? An eye cannot look directly at itself. Is the world a mirror of our mind? Sometimes it seems I can control my emotions and thoughts; other times, not.

John: Awareness is self-knowing. You are aware and you know you are aware. Just recognize that this awareness is what you are. Settle in with that. When false ideas come up based on habit, look at them from the position of your identity as presence-awareness. That is all. Simple! Then everything falls into place naturally. You recognize your true nature, and the old ideas fall away. I cannot say much more, because there is no more to say. Just keep it simple and look for yourself. Your direct experience will be its own confirmation. Read the articles on my site about others who have seen this for themselves. That may give you some encouragement.

18

Deepening Experience?

Question: I appreciated what you had to say as well as your style in delivery: mellow, direct and very eloquent! I have to say that I still have a bugaboo about the myth of the deepening experience. If it makes any sense to you, I got to thinking while you were talking, about a parallel with psychiatry (and the medical model in general), which views the client as sick, and needs to get better, versus how psychology generally views the client as 'AOK', only needing some understanding along the way.

John: What is interesting about this approach is that you are told from the start that you are utterly free, perfect and complete right now. It is hard to develop or deepen from that perspective. Unfortunately, the idea that you can deepen implies that you are not already deep enough, free enough or complete enough. So, while the idea is noble, it is really implying that you are a limited being with a problem (of not yet being deep enough). This is a flat contradiction with the basic position of the great non-duality traditions that say that there is a reality and 'thou art that'. You will need to search long and hard anywhere in these traditions that you need to 'become that' or 'deepen into that'. Strangely enough, it is those kinds of ideas that keep us from really seeing what is being pointed to. Many, many seekers are developing, deepening, awakening, purifying, stabilizing and so on. Years later, they are doing the same thing, because they do not realize that they are in a conceptual box with no exit.

19

There Are No Levels in Awareness

Question: First of all, I wanted to thank you. Your writings are excellent pointers to awareness. I have read and listened to many non-duality teachers over the past eight months and was helped by all of them. What I really like about your writings in particular was your emphasis on direct experience. In direct experience, I experience myself as awareness in waking life.

John: Right here and now you are present and aware. This is direct experience and utterly beyond doubt. 'Waking life' is just a label. What is that? Just some words appearing in the present and doubtless awareness. Recognizing your nature as that awareness itself leads to certitude and the end of suffering. It is direct self-knowledge. Following the thoughts and concepts in the mind takes you away from the immediate, direct recognition of what is clear and present in you now. Overlook that and you miss everything.

Q: But awareness seems to be lost during dreaming and deep sleep. I know conceptually that consciousness cannot be lost because it is the backdrop from which everything arises and is everything. However, I want the non-conceptual experience of this truth.

John: This is all conceptual! I encourage you to turn away from these doubts and questions. They are just being generated in thought, but they are not really relevant to the immediate non-conceptual recognition of your true nature. Your true nature is here and now. Stay with the here and now and let the other postulated states take care of themselves. If it is any consolation, you are undoubtedly present and aware in dreams. Otherwise, how do you know you had them? And you do not cease to exist when thoughts are absent, even in the waking state. Thoughts are constantly arising, changing and setting. The fact of your being remains. First see this clearly in the 'waking state'. Then this knowledge naturally covers the other states. But to hypothesize about states that are not in immediate given experience is too theoretical.

Q: I have read that there is a fourth state of consciousness, called *turiya*, which is present as a backdrop to the three other states. Therefore, one established in *turiya* no longer experiences a discontinuity when going from one of the three states to the other. The other three states are just appearances on the one awareness.

My question for you then is—how do I get to that point?

John: There is no point to get to. All that is being pointed to is awareness. You are that now. See your present identity as awareness and all the other questions will take care of themselves.

Q: Have you gotten to that point where there is no discontinuity ever? Do I just abide in the awareness and allow it to pull me deeper?

John: This is all a well-intentioned series of questions, but ultimately is based on a misunderstanding of the pointers. No harm! At least you will not have to spin on this stuff for years like I did!

Follow up ...

Q: Can you offer any additional pointers?

John: The blurb on my web site is my summary of everything I can point to using words. Take a look and see this if this resonates:

> *'Our true nature is that simple and undeniable presence of awareness that illumines all thinking, feeling and perceiving. Always present and radiantly clear, it is never obscured by time, circumstances or thoughts. The body, mind and world rise and set in awareness and have no independent existence apart from awareness. Awareness, your real being, is all there is. You are not the limited person you have taken yourself to be. Look for the separate self and you find it entirely absent. Seeing this, suffering, doubt and confusion effortlessly drop away, revealing your natural state of innate happiness and freedom. Understanding who you are is immediate and always available—here and now'.*

Q: Thanks for the reply. My direct non-conceptual experience is that I am awareness (sometimes in form, sometimes without form). However, when I go to sleep, this is lost experientially. I know intellectually that it is not lost, but my experience is that it is lost. So my problem is not a conceptual problem as you have suggested, but one of direct experience.

Further I have experienced myself directly as awareness in dreams (lucid dreaming) and have even experienced myself as awareness in the deep sleep state. However, these experiences have been rare occurrences. From this I concluded that there are more subtle levels of awareness than my current experience, and that I have had glimpses of them. So I was posing my question to you because I had imagined that being awareness during dreams and deep sleep is your direct experience, and thus you had reached a more subtle level of awareness than myself. My question to you is whether or not you directly experience yourself as awareness during the dream and deep sleep states? And if you have, how can I reach that level of awareness? If you do not, I would humbly suggest that there is a more subtle level of awareness than you and I abide as.

John: You are barking up a wrong tree here. Awareness is. Period. There are no levels or stages and nothing to get that you do not already have. Everything, including thoughts, states, waking, dreams and dreamless sleep all appear and disappear in awareness. Since awareness is here and now, there is no need to be looking for other states. It is fully present here and now. Why not look into it and discover your identity with it right now? Then that covers all the other states automatically.

Your inquiry is well intentioned but it is surely conceptual and leading you on a wild goose chase. There are no subtle levels in awareness. There are no entities such as 'you' and 'me' that have any levels of experience at all. That is your concept based on a likely misunderstanding of various things you have read. You are searching for a needle in a haystack, but unfortunately looking in the wrong haystack. You will eventually see that these seeming cogent questions are not relevant. The answer is shining right in plain view and you are not yet willing to stop all conceptual thought and see what is being pointed to. I have been down the path you are looking into for years myself and eventually found it to be useless. I am only trying to lend a hand and save you some years of effort. Believe me when I say I looked into the same issues you are investigating and found they have almost nothing to do with what the great non-dual traditions were pointing to.

Do not look for experiences. They are transitory and not worth exploring. The answer is your own being. It is here and now and ever-present. It is not an experience. Sleep and dream are just passing experiences. They are not worth much, if any, attention at all. Why give a passing thought to a passing thought?

That is about all I can say. You will have to find your own way.

Q: I appreciate your directness and respect your opinion. However, the idea of levels is not my own mental concoction based on something I misinterpreted. I have heard teachers talk and write about levels. Some speak of these levels—the individual I AM, the universal I AM and the Absolute. Others have spoken of the subtle, the causal and the super causal. And then there are those who speak of even more levels beyond those.

I am speaking from the very awareness your writings point to. Self-inquiry, the I AM mantra, pointers and kundalini-shakti energy beyond the crown chakra have taken me there. I am at peace with myself and my world. There is no suffering. But the pull to go even deeper is constantly registering on the awareness that I AM. From our correspondence it is clear that your position is that there is nothing deeper. I guess we will have to agree to disagree. I am open to the possibility that I am wrong, and that even the respected teachers who speak of levels are wrong. As you said, I must find my own way.

John: I wish you the very best in your quest.

All I can say is that after years of searching, studying the works of the most outstanding modern teachers of non-duality, talking with their surviving disciples, plus an acquaintance with the classical teachings of Vedanta and other non-dual traditions and so on.—it became clear to me that what is being pointed to is a timeless and ever-present reality that is utterly beyond the concept of levels and stages. These ideas are conclusively refuted by the historical traditions in their most essential representations.

You may also come to see a simple fact. All stages and levels are imagined in awareness. They are all contained in awareness. Levels and stages imply time and space and someone to traverse them. All these are concepts imagined within awareness. Awareness is timeless and spaceless. It is the non-dual reality itself. Everything is that. There is only that. Once it is seen that there is only one, non-dual reality, then the ideas of time and space and levels of attainment all collapse. It is all pure imagination. It seems compelling until questioned.

Being-awareness is what is real. That is what you are. There are no levels in it because it is utterly timeless, spaceless, partless and one-without-a-second. How could levels apply to the one, non-dual reality? Some call reality the clear space of emptiness. How can there be levels in that which is empty and contentless?

Time and space are created in the mind in thought. They are imaginary concepts. There can be no levels without time and space, which are purely mind-created concepts. That is why stages and levels are completely imaginary, like a dream. Dreams appear real—until questioned. I would recommend that you stick to very clear and time-tested teachings and also use your own reason and clear thinking.

Finally, no matter where you go and how many levels you achieve, you can never move away from the fact of your identity as presence-awareness. It is simply a changeless, irrefutable truth. All experiences are passing images on the changeless awareness that you are. Existence does not become more existent, awareness does not become more awareness, love does not become more love, your identity as that does not become more identical, the utter non-existence of a separate self does not become more absent.

I assure you that the great teachers of non-dual traditions had no interest at all in levels of attainment. This is a historical fact, backed up by recorded teachings and from personal testimony. I am not denying your experience, though, and I encourage you to seek out the deepest truth of your heart. If you do, you cannot possibly go wrong.

If you have not done so, check out the works of Nisargadatta Maharaj (especially, *I AM THAT*) and Ramana Maharshi (for example, *Talks with Ramana Maharshi*). These are considered to be two of the best teachers of modern times. While you are at it, you may want to look into the teachings of 'Sailor' Bob Adamson. You may be surprised at what you find the essential teachings of non-duality to be. They are nothing like the popularized version of spiritual paths that most of us are familiar with.

Q: I see truth in what you are saying and will check out the works you have recommended. I appreciate the advice.

20

Separation, Individuality and Suffering

Question: I still have a sense of separation and individuality, which makes me feel that the final and full realization of true beingness has not really taken place.

John: It is good that you bring this up and get the issue out in the open for some investigation. For years, I was involved in meditation and non-dual philosophy and somehow the basics were elusive to me. This notion that we are some kind of separate individual apart from the reality can still be operative at some level. It is really an idea, an assumption. Yet it brings in its wake a sense of separation. And then all the seeking, grasping and identification arises in the mind in an attempt to fix the perceived problem. It is good to have this whole mechanism exposed in the light of clear seeing. It is actually fairly simple, but we rarely hear this presented clearly and simply.

The notion of an existent separate individual and our identity as that is driving the whole conceptual apparatus. We imagine ourselves to be separate from the reality. But the reality is pointed out as the sense of being-awareness itself, not as some abstraction, but as our everyday, ordinary sense of presence-awareness. When this gets pointed out there can be some sense of the simplicity and availability of it. Then you look to see if this presence-awareness is something apart from you. A little looking shows this is not so. This is what you are and always have been. As this strikes home, you can appreciate the implications of what this presence-awareness is, its nature, its availability, and your present and effortless identity as this. Still, the habit of imagining separation and the consequent doubts and questions may linger in the mind, through force of habit. So, it is good to have a clear understanding of what is going on in order take this by the roots and unwind things at the source.

Here are some points to consider. All suffering is just arising in thought. Suffering thoughts all revolve around a sense of a separate self. So, suffering equals self-centered thoughts. Self-centered thoughts are dependent upon the belief in an existing separate self, and our assumed identity with that. This separate self is assumed to be present, rather than known to be present. This assumption is the driver of all suffering. It gets pointed out that there is no separate self at all, and we are encouraged to look in our direct experience to see if it is present. Looking for any separate self and not finding it uproots the belief in it. So, the light of awareness is turned directly onto the imagined separate self to see if it is present. Discovering that there is no separate 'I' present in our experience completely dismantles the core of self-centered thinking. All the doubts, questions, seeking and suffering are undercut because the root driver is exposed. And still you cannot deny your clear and unshakable identity as the open and clear presence of being-awareness, which is utterly beyond doubt.

This approach is very practical and yields tangible and clear results. Nothing is gained, but the network of self-centered concepts is removed, and that is the only problem there ever was. Even that is more of an optical illusion because we have never left the presence of what we are. Separation never happened. Clear and direct looking reveals this to be true. It is important to apply the pointers and verify in your own direct experience what is being pointed out.

21

Awareness and the Mind

Question: I am wondering if you could spell out in a little more detail your understanding of the two aspects of recognition you sometimes mention, namely, recognizing that you are non-dual awareness and uprooting the cause of suffering. You mention in your book that there is often a back and forth settling in period during which people report that spacious awareness is self transparent for awhile and then opaque when the mind is fixated on something (wavering between awareness and the mind). According to your understanding, how do you understand the difference between awareness and mind?

John: To me awareness refers to the non-conceptual sense of pure knowing itself. It is ever-present and clear and beyond doubt. It has nothing to do with thinking. Then there is the mind, which is conceptual thought or simply thought. Ultimately, awareness and the mind are one because there can be no thought apart from awareness. Awareness is the substance of which thought is fabricated. To imagine thought as an independent something separate from awareness, and more importantly to imagine ourselves as something apart from awareness, is the only real issue. That forms the root of all imaginary suffering and bondage. To rectify this matter decisively through clear seeing ends all questions, doubts and suffering.

Q: What wavers back and forth?

John: The focus of our attention wanders into false beliefs.

The ever clear awareness never leaves at all. It is just that we overlook it and focus on shadows. But even those shadows are arising and setting in the clear presence of awareness. Once this is seen, the wavering ends. This can be seen and resolved directly, once we are clear on what is being pointed out.

Q: Is there a preference for one state over the other (for example, focusing on thought or not focusing on thought)?

John: Once you see what is going on, there is no difference. Awareness is ever-present and you never leave it. Seeing this is the end of the wavering.

Q: Is there a benefit to cultivating a habit of dwelling in/as awareness rather than thought?

John: Habits and cultivation are supported in the mind. They cannot go on except as a conceptual activity, and so they are apt to reinforce the basic error. Awareness cannot be practiced. That is just the fact of it. All practices are from the point of view of the imagined separate entity and must be abandoned in the end. Remember, this is the natural state, not the maintenance state!

Q: Do you see this habit as something easily attainable?

John: It is totally unnecessary. You just need to see the facts. Understanding is everything. Practice is a much less effective approach. The recognition of your identity is the ultimate understanding.

Q: How is the cause of suffering uprooted?

John: By tracing it to its root, which is a wrong belief, and uprooting the wrong belief through clear seeing. Ignorance is eradicated through knowledge. It is all about understanding, not doing anything. The belief that you are a doer is the root misconception anyhow. You are totally non-existent as a separate entity.

Q: How is the deep understanding (and not a mere intellectual understanding) achieved?

John: Through a penetrating examination to see if a separate self is present, not as a speculation, but as an actual looking or seeing in direct experience. Thinking and seeing are completely different. It is like reading the menu and eating the food. Most spiritual seekers, due to confusion, are eating the menu.

Q: In your understanding, how are the approaches we have been discussing related?

John: They go together like two wings of a bird. It is a tandem approach that clearly reveals what is real in you and dismantles the root suffering, which is the belief that you exist as a separate self apart from the real. This usually does not strike home by reading about it. It seems to be accessible more clearly, in practical life, through living contact and dialogue. We invariably try to 'get this' as if it were a mental recognition. But it has nothing to do with the mind. So unless we have a living example, we tend to fall back into a conceptual understanding. That was my experience anyway.

22

The Imaginary, Separate Doer

Question: It is quite sometime since I last had contact. Life is much quieter these days! Questions still occasionally float by, that get me hooked, so I hope you do not mind if I ask a couple.

John: Just remember that questions are for the mind. They are not a problem really. However, your true nature is not questionable. It is clearly present and beyond doubt. The clear understanding of your nature is the solution and resolves all doubts.

Q: Recently my son started to go to nursery, which I pay for with my income from work. Since he started, my work has gone very quiet, and at the moment I cannot pay his fees (my husband is now paying for them). In a situation like this normally I would feel I should be doing everything I possibly can to improve my business. But I am not doing any of that. I feel that I cannot be bothered. No matter how much I try to push myself, nothing happens. I find that it is getting stressful.

John: There are lots of 'I' and 'my' references here! The sense of being an 'I' doing everything is where the stickiness comes in. Are you beating your heart, breathing your lungs, creating your thoughts or running the show at all? To take a stand as an imaginary, separate 'doer' puts a separation into the picture. This is the root of all stress, ultimately. Once the separation is created (in thought), then there are various ideas that we have to fix things.

Without that belief, life flows along. Actions come up to be done, but there is very little problem. Things happen or they do not. The mind does what it does to make decisions and so on, but you stand in peace in a deeper place of harmony.

Q: Is it sometimes the case that when this is seen through that we may still have to do things that we really do not want to be doing?

John: The idea that 'we' are in there doing and not doing is the primary source of conflict. But have you ever really found a separate self at all? When we say 'I', 'me', and 'we' who are we talking about? You are the ultimate self, the very ground of the universe, peaceful and free. Not seeing this is the problem. There is no real solution without taking things to their roots and resolving the basic issue of your real identity. Then all the mental issues fall away because they are based on a misunderstanding.

Q: There still at times feels like a lot of mental conflict is going on from trying to make it all work.

John: Without the belief of being something we are not, life goes on with much less effort and conflict. All the conflict is just various thoughts and ideas in the mind. It is all self-centered thinking based on an imaginary sense of who we are and what we need to be happy.

Q: My husband now thinks we should not have the baby monitor on at night, and I absolutely disagree, so there is tension trying to work this out between us. I know this all sounds like very petty stuff, but I just get stuck on issues like this and would love some feedback.

John: My advice is to get clear on the basic issue of who and what you are. When you clear up your basic identity, there are very few issues left to deal with. Then everything just comes up to be done without any reference to a separate someone. The imagined separation disappears and the mind is not fighting with itself or other people. Everything goes on as before, but there is no taking anything personally, because there is no person in the picture in the way that we have conceived it. You need nothing. You need to do nothing. And nothing anyone does can really affect your deeper source of joy. As someone said once, life becomes a game to play in all of its infinite variety.

23

I Can Stop the Search

Question: I attended your talk tonight at East-West Bookstore and spoke with you for a moment afterwards. I really wanted to thank you, because you managed to cut through the crap for me in a couple of short hours. I have been at this for many years—about twenty-five, actually—but something really shifted for me hearing you talk. I wrote a journal entry about the experience I had tonight and I would love to share it with you, but I wanted to get your permission before sending it. In a nutshell, I got that everything could be dropped. All I have to do is nothing about it at all. I can stop the search because the search is false. The search cannot get to what is real, because only 'nothing but being' is real. The search is something. Everything is something. And I can give it all up. I can give up everything.

I came into your talk tonight seeking enlightenment, and I left knowing I already had it. What a gift. Thank you very much. I would love to have an email or telephone discussion with you to clear out any remaining doubts. I am not even sure I have any remaining doubts. Thank you again for sharing the great tradition in such a concise and contemporary way.

Follow up ...

Q: I just do not know how to express to you my gratitude. It is so funny, right now, knowing the search is over. Knowing today was the day. And now ... life happens! Thanks again, John, for helping me so much. I had no idea anything would come of me driving to Mountain View that night. But there was something very magical about meeting you. Though I am not putting you (as a separate person) on a pedestal or anything, I think that gratitude will always be there.

John: Everything has beautifully revealed itself. No doubts about that! It is really nice to see this understanding open up for you. You are as I was. I had a lot of acquired knowledge and experiences but just needed a few pointers and the encouragement to have faith in my own experience. That is what Bob Adamson's pointers did for me. If our interaction has been a catalyst for you, then I am very happy with that.

24

Apart from Thoughts, Problems Do Not Exist

Question: I find myself in a bit of quandary and would be grateful for any advice that you can give me. I have been seeking since my early teens and, more recently, investigating various teachers presenting the approach of non-duality. I have been avidly reading the books and listening to the talks given by a couple of prominent teachers every day for over a year. I have also attended a few retreats and talks.

I now find that the impasse that I felt for years is getting stronger, and I am not getting any closer to letting go of this 'me' and realizing the truth about presence-awareness. However, I understand intellectually that these thoughts are rising in presence-awareness and my not getting it is also presence-awareness, and so on. I have had for a number of years some sort of continual background empty, aching feeling which has grown stronger over the past ten months or so. It is really pissing me off! I have been trying to trace this back and identify where this is arising from, who it belongs too and who is the 'I' that thinks it has a problem and so on. But to no avail. This is really driving me mad! I really feel like packing all the reading and searching in, but I know that it has got hold of me and I cannot let this go until I realize that I have never left it

John: You are making things much too complicated. If you are finding yourself hanging around this for more than a few weeks or months, you are missing some of the basic points. I found for myself that the reading and listening had limits. The key, if the basic understanding is not clear, is to enter into living dialog.

I will not repeat all the basic points, as they are covered

on my site and in my book. The main thing is to see that all these issues are just thoughts in the mind. Apart from those thoughts, the problems do not exist. It is the mind generating the problems and looking for answers. But there are no answers at that level because the mind and its assumptions are where the root of the problem lies.

The answer is the non-conceptual recognition of your true nature, which is ever clear as the undeniable sense of presence-awareness. That is it in a nutshell. All doubts, suffering and problems, including attaining spiritual realization are just concepts. These concepts all revolve around an imaginary sense of self. There is no resolve until the sense of self is thoroughly examined and discarded. This is an active inquiry and will not 'happen' without a clear understanding of what is at work.

All your problems and doubts are based on a misperception and until you clear that up, you will keep spinning. All the self-centered thoughts depend on the belief in a separate self. But there is not one anywhere in the picture. Have you found one yet? If there is no one there, then the basis of all the suffering is not present and the course is run.

25

The Antidote to Suffering

Question: Perhaps the most precious gift of the understanding is the absence of any further need to prove that I understand or 'there is understanding here', as I formerly would so carefully say to try to prove to someone (me!) that I am absent!

John: All I would say is the following, which is just a summary of some basic points. You exist and you are aware. What you sought and needed to know was only ever this. This is what you are. It is easily verifiable and cannot be doubted. All teachers and books, if they are worth their salt, are pointing to what you are. Therefore, once this is understood, they all become redundant.

Suffering. Few get to clarity on this and really understand it. Without this coming into crystal clear focus, the searching, seeking and suffering go on, in spite of however much else is understood. Suffering is whatever doubts, problems, issues, questions and concepts arise that bring us trouble in the mind and heart. It could be lying in bed at 3 o'clock in the morning wondering 'Why am I such a good-for-nothing lonely schmuck?' When looked at closely, these are all thoughts. Without thoughts, these have no existence. Suffering is a subset of thoughts. This leads those with only a partial appreciation to try to stop or get rid of thinking. This is totally fruitless, as it is just more mental noise and is itself just another movement of thought.

All thought is not suffering, only a subset of thoughts. What are those thoughts? They are thoughts that revolve around 'me' or 'myself'. Suffering is nothing less or more than self-centered thoughts. No self-centered thoughts means no suffering. The root of all self-centered thoughts (the cause) is the idea of a separate 'I. That root notion, that I ever existed as a thing apart from presence-awareness, was the beginning of the rise of suffering and separation. All identities, concepts, beliefs, labels and so on. that fall under the category of self-centered thoughts are just ideas attached to this root belief. Once the notion of separation was believed in, we spent a lifetime trying to solidify this imagined notion through believing in the mind's self-created concepts ('I am not good enough', 'I am not enlightened', 'Now I have it', 'Now I do not', 'Others are there, I am not' and so on). It is all a fraud, because it is all talking in terms of a defective, isolated and separate self, which we have taken as true.

The antidote is simple, elegant and profound. It is to question whether there is or ever has been any such thing as a separate self. If it exists, it must be present and observable. Where is it? Can it be seen or found in direct experience? On the other hand, can you ever find yourself as something separate and apart from existence-awareness? Is there a separate person at all in the picture? Has there ever been one? Presence-awareness, in direct experience, is pure clarity, peace and wholeness. There is not a single thing wrong with it, and it does not need to be fixed. And this, upon close examination, is what you are. It is not an attainment, but a fact that simply needs to be verified. It is easy to hear this and not fully apply what is being pointed to.

See all suffering, doubt and confusion as simply a movement of thought and nothing else. See such thoughts as simply stories or tales of a poor, separate and defective 'me'—in other words, self-centered thoughts. All of these thoughts depend on the existence of a presumed entity that we have assumed for so long to be present that we do not even question that it may be totally absent. To look for this presumed separate one and see, really see, that there is nothing there, will completely pull the plug on self-centered thinking because the root cause, the presumed presence of the 'me', is questioned. It has survived through non-inquiry.

If you look through all this, get a glimpse of clarity and come out with 'Now I am there', you have completely missed the whole point. That is just another self-centered thought for someone who thinks he is now 'there'. This is a subtle trap that is easy to fall into. This whole thing is not a prize to obtain or some goal to reach. With this attitude, the sense of separate self comes right back in the back door and proudly announces his absence: the fabled 'enlightened ego'. The proof that this does not work is that the suffering and doubts and questions keep coming, because the root has not really been severed.

Grasp the matter of suffering by the horns and really apply it in direct experience. The net result is that the suffering, seeking, worshipping teachers and searching for techniques comes to a halt. There is no one out there who can give us anything that is not already present in us right now. One of the signs that this has struck home will be an aversion to putting anyone, including yourself, on a pedestal. With no one there, there is no one to put on or remove from a pedestal!

Q: Thank you for this latest unexpected and most welcome summary of the basics. I find it beautifully accurate, especially with regard to the traps I fall into. It seems simple and elegant, a perfect fit for where I find myself now, as this all settles in and the looking seems more natural and less contrived.

26

The Non-Existence of the Person

Question: Now and again I pop onto your website to read some of the correspondence on the articles page. I was reading one article and the questioner was describing being aware of physical sensations and then seeing the 'I' appearing to apparently take ownership of that sensation (that is, the conceptualization process occurring). He went on to describe other things, which resonated with me (Mike). I noticed the similar experiences between two individuals. Then it suddenly hit me, Mike and this other guy are just imaginary characters. It is as if the idea of one character validates or substantiates the idea of another character, and hence the dream of individuality is assumed to be real.

John: It is excellent that you see this. This is the centerpiece of the puzzle that many overlook, even after years of exploring spiritual teachings.

Q: It was as if a silent explosion went off, a recognition that what was appearing presently was in fact a play, which appears to be so real or convincing. It is ironic or somewhat strange that apparent individuals have the same apparent unfolding in the story or gradual recognition of their true nature. What a beautiful story it is! I can only say that the point of the story is to see the sheer pointlessness of it. It is simply a story. And it is only an aspect of what I truly am, which is that which is aware of the story. It is clearly seen now how even reading the articles themselves can validate the story of personhood, but more and more the story is seen for what it is.

John: Whether the story has a point or does not is still just an opinion in the mind. The main fact, that you have seen, is that the character at the center of it is completely imaginary. To see your nature clearly as that doubtless sense of existence, which is present and aware, is key. However, to truly see the non-existence of the person that we have imagined ourselves to be is vital, because this is the source of the questions, doubts and problems. All questions, doubts and problems are for someone. When that someone is discovered as a fiction, all these things are uprooted because the root cause is found to be absent. I am glad to hear that all of this is registering.

Q: The 'I' can never know it …

John: How can an imaginary, non-existent entity know anything? The 'I' is just a thought, and a thought cannot know awareness because it is an object in awareness.

Q: … but it can be it.

John: Well, that is what you are. And now you know!

27

Awareness and Deep Sleep

Question: What happens to presence-awareness during sleep or deep sleep? Would you address this topic?

John: It does not go anywhere. The second the alarm rings or someone calls your name, you hear it and wake up. You must be present, and awareness must be there. Otherwise, how could you wake up upon hearing something? It is just that the mind and senses are in abeyance temporarily. Life goes on! That is the short answer!

Revelations and Changes

Question: It has been nine days since we met at your Saturday workshop. These nine days have been an awesome series of revelations and changes for me. I would like to mention a few of these.

John: I would love to hear what is up.

Q: I have discovered that there are no more agendas. There are no agendas with my girlfriend, writing books, dieting and so forth. Agendas and expectations have mostly vanished. Consequently, life presents one adventurous surprise after another.

John: Once the simplicity of the pointing strikes home that what we are seeking we already are, then the expectations and agendas that we used to put on the appearances start to drop out of the focus. We are no longer looking 'out there' for something to make us happy or whole or complete. There is more spontaneity, less living from the perspective of a defective person who needs something to be a certain way. The truth is that life is always arising as a series of spontaneous events anyway, but we were living from the point of view of a separate person trying to control the events. This was never true and created a lot of resistance and suffering.

Q: I am present with myself much more. Agitated or joyful or depressed feelings are much more fully expressed. There are fewer 'shoulds' and 'should nots' related to expressing emotions or feelings. I am mainly out in front, paradoxically without any need to express whatever comes up. I can even be brusque now, something quite new for me. Gratefully, I exhibit more humor about my various woes and stories.

John: Yes, you are more natural and less concerned with your own internal landscape of thoughts and feelings as well. Those also are seen as part of the flow of the spontaneous functioning without having to reference them to a sense of self. They are no longer 'ours' but just part of the expression. The stories are just seen for what they are—mental creations about a fictional character that we used to take for ourselves. There is a lot less belief put into them. With the belief taken out they tend to subside because there is no more serious energy going into them.

Q: You might remember how I described Dzogchen's (a type of Tibetan Buddhism) two-step commands. First, be aware of any object or thought. Second, be aware of your awareness of that object or thought. After the second command, one or more of five attributes arise: peace, silence, luminosity, expanded awareness of space and context and expanded presence. I recall you commenting that these tastes or flavors of awareness of course do occur, but that no two-stage technique is required to access them. Since our session, I am more frequently aware of awareness and experiencing these attributes. No technique seems necessary.

John: The main thing is to see that awareness is not a technique. It is a natural and present fact. That awareness, which is your actual being, has its own flavor and characteristics. You just begin to look into that and see what is there. There is a natural curiosity to explore this. I find that making it into a technique brings in the mind and too much of a goal orientation. Sometimes that obscures the naturalness and simplicity of things.

Q: I quit reading spiritual books and meditating. If you recall, I described a certain meditation technique I had been using, and I asked you if that fell within your description of a practice that subtly reinforces the 'I'. You said, 'Yes, it does'. At present, I feel zero need to continue that meditation technique.

John: With the dawning of the recognition of your true nature the activities will come to balance and whatever needs to adjust will do so. Certain things may drop away or not. Just follow your heart and your natural intelligence. Once you get to the essence of things, much of the supporting structures that we used to rely on are less useful and interesting. You need to use your own judgment as there is no prescription for this.

Q: John, I cannot find any steady 'I' within 'my' mind. If it pops up, at least during the daytime, it is obviously merely a fragmentary, illusionary thought. When I lay down to sleep, the 'I' fires up again with fantasies of 'my' greatness as a twenty-three year old Major General during World War Two or a similar grandiose story. Your recommended inquiries slow down this mental onslaught, but do not eliminate it entirely. During the day, I am largely free of the 'I'.

John: The belief in being a separate 'I' was fed for many years. It is something of a habit. It may continue to pop up. However, once you have questioned it, you can never really give it the same emphasis as before. All it is, is a habitual thought pattern arising and setting in the clear presence of awareness that you are. Just see that thoughts cannot be there without you. And whether they arise or not does not really touch your essence. From this understanding things naturally come into balance. Do not make thought into an enemy. It is really a lifeless shadow with no real power.

Q: I clearly see the origin of rampant emotionality of human beings. This little critter 'I' is what runs them around. Therefore, for the last week, I have seldom taken things personally, and when I do, that personalizing lasts only a short time. It is now obvious that I have nothing to do with others' reactions, just as they have nothing to do with mine.

John: Excellent insight.

Q: At the same time, I am discerning more clearly what I want—and do not want—around me.

John: A natural intelligence kicks in and you may find yourself expressing yourself and your interests in different ways that align with what your deeper understanding and feelings of your heart resonate with.

Q: I am now clear about my own teaching. In my classes, attendees learn to witness their inner worlds, pick out the predominant core unconscious belief, watch it appearing over and over in gross and subtle ways in their everyday lives, and make quite different choices. Greater clarity, energy, and freedom take over. Some participants make enormous changes. I now understand this level of instruction might be called 'level one'. It is useful and practical, but it fails to fully reveal the natural state. Your teaching bypasses level one by clarification of 1) our true nature as presence-awareness and 2) the falsity of any 'I' existing. In short, I no longer can teach the way I have been doing. It is not appealing to me.

John: The old approaches may come in for a re-evaluation. We always end up communicating what is nearest and dearest to our hearts. I would say just go with what is natural and what comes up spontaneously to do.

Q: I am reading your book in a manner new to me. I read for about ten or fifteen minutes of insights and then put it down. I never pick it up thinking, 'This might hold the answer I have been looking for'. Instead, I already know the 'answer'—awareness-presence. What the text creates is continuous realizations about the diverse misdirections concocted by the 'I'. Reading the book seems like dialoguing with you. It is a superb book, truly unique.

John: I am glad the book is resonating. What is most important is the presence of your own understanding of what is being pointed to. If the book helps to support that, that is fine. With the basics in clear view, you can look at books or not or visit teachers or not, but they will not really be able to tell you anything you do not already know for yourself.

29

Awakening and the Natural State

Question: Some approaches talk about a first step of awakening and then a settling into the natural state. What is your view on this?

John: All the talk about steps is misleading. I do not really go in for the dichotomy of awakening versus the natural state. I do not even like to talk about awakening, because it is such a buzz word and really gets the imagination going! The natural state of presence-awareness is here now. It is clear and available. It is not an awakening or attainment at all. It is already the case, but has been overlooked. I find the talk of awakening to be very misleading. So, I would say to forget about the steps and processes and just come back to the simple recognition of what is already clear and present.

30

How Do You Handle Someone's Reactivity?

Question: My girlfriend has been passing through several quite hard trials. I listen, ask questions, listen some more, comment where appropriate and tell her about the uselessness of the mind and the necessity to examine her suffering. She seems to partly catch on, but does not respond fully to my comments. I can handle about forty-fifty minutes of her suffering talk, and then it becomes a hot desert wind beating on me. Actually, I no longer take her talk personally. I do not identify with it at all. I am not responsible for her situations. I have zero desire to become a therapist. There is not a lot of 'me' that takes in this talk and thrashes around in circles about it. Nevertheless, the body-mind seems to be assaulted by it—much as it would be burned by a hot desert wind.

Recently I told her, 'You have five minutes to express suffering, and no more. Then, if you want, I will be pleased to listen to any inquiry into the suffering'. For me, the appropriate response to suffering-talk is (1) compassion, (2) steadfast speaking out about, and demonstration of, genuine inquiry about suffering and (3) putting a real limit to suffering-talk, for both our sakes. I have not done number three long enough to describe any effects. Maybe you have something other to offer. How do you handle someone's reactivity and refusal to examine his or herself? Do you have any suggestion when a close friend or mate goes on and on?

John: What I have found is that we cannot determine the experience of others. They are going to be as they are. They have their own unique way of expression that needs to be respected. You may or may not resonate with that and may even end up stating very clearly what you are willing to put up with! What I have learned is that this approach to understanding ourselves is really an individual affair (for lack of a better word). The main thing is that we continue to look at the basics and find clarity for ourselves. Everything comes to balance from there.

The idea that someone else should see this, or not suffer or be less reactive can bring in a needless division. They either will or they won't and there is not a damn thing you, I or anyone else can do about it. All you can do is point, but you cannot motivate someone else to see or cause them to see. That is just the way it works. If there is a resonance and response, great. If not, that is fine, too. You cannot make people want to be free of suffering. They have to come to it in their own time.

In the meantime, you can make sure that you are clear about what you are willing to put up with and respond accordingly. Then it becomes your own issue to deal with, rather than playing a waiting game in response to someone else's agenda. The desire to change others is a trap, really. Even worse is to make our happiness dependent on them changing. Your happiness has no relation to what other people do or not do. Make sure to see this. Then whatever they do or not is really fine.

Another key thing is not to see someone as flawed or limited. Like everyone, they are also that constant state of being-awareness, even if the mind of suffering is present—just as with ourselves! There is no need to put a lot of reaction and concern into the reality of their thoughts and suffering.

Make sure you see your own true nature in spite of whatever is coming up in the mind. Also see others in the same way. If you view someone else as a problematic, defective person, that only exacerbates the illusion that they are already believing in.

31

Chasing Experiences

Question: I am currently working my way through your book. I seem to have caught this non-dualism virus, and I cannot get rid of it. I came to you through reading and listening to your teacher, 'Sailor' Bob. I currently do not have someone in the role of a guide to help me through some tangles, so I decided to write to you. Three months earlier, when I began to take these teachings seriously, I had moments where I had some wonderful clarity about these teachings. These experiences were relatively short, and I would quickly drift back into object/thought identification. Since then, I have been trying to chase these experiences by reading more and more books, listening to tapes and so on., but I cannot seem to recapture that original wonder and spaciousness I experienced. In fact, my efforts seem to be making matters worse!

John: Yes, because all of this is looking precisely away from what is being pointed to. Your natural identity of being-awareness is not in books, tapes or teachers! You are not an experience. You are that presence in which experiences arise and set. If you look for experiences, you will go astray. Instead, look into him to whom the experiences are occurring. Awareness is already free, clear and spacious. You just need to recognize it.

Q: What on one day can make amazing sense when I read it, on another other day seems like it is written in Chinese. Or else it appears like some sort of tricky intellectual wordplay. Is this normal?

John: It is if you are still looking to the mind and trying to get the answer there. But you cannot!

Q: This felt sense just will not stabilize, and I am afraid I am simply turning this understanding into another waste of time.

John: You cannot stabilize the answer in the mind. Awareness, which is what you are, does not need to be stabilized. It is already stable. It is the unchanging reality itself. It is already present. Looking to the mind or to an experience is an exercise in futility because those are always changing. But that awareness that is knowing the mind—what about that? Give that some attention to see what that is. And are you apart from that?

32

Acceptance Does Not Really Work

Question: My question is the word 'acceptance'. I understand that awareness is all. Bodies and minds appear that have conditioning and programming and the 'me' attitude. Yet, it is all awareness doing this. The conditioning has been a lot of trouble for me and others. To say 'accept conditioning' is a scary thing. It seems like it will continue on because of acceptance. Can you clear this up for me?

John: I certainly do not say accept conditioning! Why accept the source of suffering? Suffering is just the expression of habitual thoughts based on a wrong view of who we are. As you may recall, I said the suffering is just habitual thoughts appearing in the mind. When closely examined these turn out to be thoughts based on a limited sense of self, or self-centered thoughts. These are based on a false sense of being a separate 'I' apart from what is true and real. The whole tree of suffering sprouts from this root. But it is a wrong belief. To investigate this belief and expose it as false is to undercut the whole network of suffering in a profound way. The habitual suffering thoughts are drained of their power. Then the natural state of clear presence-awareness is evident. And this is what you truly are. That is an overview.

There is not a separate self at all. So there is no one present to accept or not accept. That is why acceptance does not really work in the long run. Acceptance is more of a technique. This approach deals more with clear understanding of things rather than techniques.

33

Do Not Seek a No-Thought State

Question: Over the past month, I have been slowly soaking-in your book *Awakening to the Natural State*, reading just a few pages each night. There is heart-felt appreciation for the clarity in your book. For close to two years, I had become immersed in books by Nisargadatta Maharaj, Ramana Maharshi, 'Sailor' Bob Adamson, Tony Parsons and others. I am now at the point where the desire to devour these texts has nearly vanished.

John: You have honed in on some really good pointers, for the most part. But, as you are coming to see, the answer is not in the books!

Q: When encountering a short passage in your book or a poem by Rumi, for example, it has gotten to the point where I usually fall into a no-thought state in which the mind falls silent. I do not know the significance of this state or how to compare it with other such states.

John: Do not fall into the trap that this has anything to do with a silent mind. It does not! Your true nature remains and is present whether thoughts are present or not. Once you see this, you do not pay attention to the mind at all. You are looking into your true nature, not the mind or its states. This is a key issue that many are not clear on.

Q: There is also a feeling of being on the cusp of seeing what awakening is. At the same time, it is clear that it is not here yet.

John: In the end 'awakening' is a totally worthless concept! Many seekers are chasing concepts such as enlightenment and awakening. They are tantalizing concepts to the mind, but unrelated to genuine self-knowledge. What you are is already present and aware and needs no awakening at all. It is simply discovering what is already present but overlooked.

Q: There is a falling out of this no-thought state when I have to work, respond to my young childrens' needs or take care of pressing errands.

John: This is because you have been led to believe (incorrectly) that the essential matter has to do with a no-thought state. Give up this false idea and things will get much simpler.

Q: I have noted from you and from others who have experienced awakening that books rarely take one over the razor's edge.

John: I do not claim any such thing as awakening, so do not put me into a box with those who have had such things! There is no razor's edge and nothing to get over! This is still postulating that there is something 'out there' that you do not have. This is still a concept and a false one at that. You are already what you are. You just need to have a look. All the spiritual verbiage we have gotten from books ends up leading us astray in the end.

Q: Let me ask you a very practical question. Does watching Bob Adamson on video, for example, or listening to Tony Parsons on CD, help with breaking-through, or is the final break-through almost always only accomplished by way of a physical, in-person interaction with someone who has realized?

John: Again, give up this idea of breaking through and so on. With this concept, you are off looking for something you imagine you do not have. You are the answer you are seeking. However, if the basic simplicity of this is not clear, it can be good to talk it over with someone with a clear understanding of this. They only point to what is clear and present within you. Of the people you mention, I found Bob Adamson to be particularly clear and effective. If you feel you are still missing something, which you are not (!), you can certainly talk to someone who can point you back to the essence of things.

Q: I very much appreciate your insights, John.

John: Stay in touch if you feel like it.

34

Stay with What Is Clear, Simple and Present

Question: I have really been looking at the 'I' or 'me', as you suggested. I am forced to conclude that they are simply words to describe a particular body in order to distinguish it from another. It does not seem possible to locate an entity named 'I'. I understand that the word is not the thing. One could refer to oneself as 'Je' or 'Yo', and it would not make any difference. The past memories that are associated with the 'I' concept are just fragments of experiences that the body has been subjected to. They come and go quite automatically and are beyond control. I am not any particular one of these thought streams.

John: All very clearly seen.

Q: The problem is that they constantly steal attention, much like a thief, and create involvement and, hence, discomfort.

John: Only because they are believed in. We take them to be real and then attend to them. There is still some idea that the self-centered thoughts might bring some happiness or security. However, this is flawed for two reasons. First, there is no self to which they apply, so the whole thing is a house of cards. Second, happiness, security and peace come from your real nature, which is the presence-awareness upstream of thought. This remains completely free and untouched by the mind at all times. Once this is clear, all the interest in the mind dissipates naturally. We simply see that the answer is not in the mind. The attention ceases to go into empty belief patterns.

Q: Understanding this, I can usually snap myself out of it before things gain too much momentum.

John: Just come back to seeing what is clear and present. See your real nature as it is, and you will not have to deal with the mind. Does the sun need to deal with the clouds? However, if self-centered thoughts come up you can also deconstruct them, as follows. Notice that suffering is simply self-centered thoughts. Self-centered thoughts are descriptions of a limited self. Direct looking reveals there is nothing like a separate self at all. This pulls the juice right out of the heart the storm, so to speak.

Q: I do realize that the only thing that I could be is simple conscious presence, which illuminates everything that happens, including the thinking. It is like a subtle fragrance which gives hints of peace and beauty, but often seems distant.

John: Yes, beautifully put. Continue to get to know this. It appears subtle and even distant because we have not given it its proper attention. We have focused primarily on the mind. Now let the looking come back to your true nature, which is simple presence-awareness—undeniable, effortless presence-awareness. It is so simple that we overlook it.

Q: I know there is something not quite right about my description, because awareness does not seem to be describable!

John: No word is it. But can you deny your own conscious being? It is direct, non-conceptual knowing of what is present and aware in you. You are that.

Q: Would it be better just to disbelieve all thoughts and descriptions, since they are never adequate anyway and only seem to create more involvement?

John: Yes, that is a good approach. Just turn back from the labeling process of the mind and see what experience is like outside of that process. Your real being has nothing to do with labels and ideas.

Q: I have read your book and most of the articles, and I really like them. I can feel that they are pointing me in the right direction, but it is not absolutely real at this point.

John: Your own presence, your own awareness—is that real or an illusion? Do not go looking for something that you do not have. Stay with what is clear, simple and present. You are what you are seeking. Just get clear on what you are and forget all the looking and searching for something that is not present.

Your own being, which is present and brightly aware, is it. All the words, due to ignorance and not knowing any better, tend to take us away from the simplicity of it. Let this sink in. The focus on the thoughts will subside, and the clarity and freedom inherent in your true nature will emerge naturally. It has worked for many others, and it will work for you too!

35

There Is No Need to Be Aware of Awareness

Question: I have read the article on suffering many times and have clearly seen the mechanism. Currently I need reminding of my true nature and use a question that you pose a lot: 'Am I present and aware right now?' My awareness comes back to presence-awareness. I see that I can never leave presence awareness, because everything arises in that, but I need this prompt, right now, to be aware of it. I am not waiting for anything to happen and have no expectations about this. I am just happy to come back as often as I can to this awareness.

John: Probe into this issue of 'coming back to awareness'. It is not really true that you leave it and come back to it. It can be very powerful to consider the basic Question: 'Do I ever leave it?' If I do not, then there is no more need for remembering it or coming back to it. Ultimately, this is the maintenance-free, natural state. You can explore any remaining concepts about separation from awareness and any need to come back to it. There is no need to be aware of awareness because you are awareness itself. These are just residual unexamined beliefs. A little investigation will expose these, leaving you in the clear recognition of what you always are. It is completely effortless and needs no maintenance at all.

36

Teachers, Books and Seeking

Question: I ordered your book a few weeks ago. There is a straightforwardness in your communication. There seems to be a complete lack of obfuscation that reached me and made me want to write to you.

I had an experience last July which completely re-routed me. I was involved with a technique call Pathwork, which is a spiritual/emotional/psychological approach to healing various kinds of life trauma and dysfunction. In the middle of the session, the 'me' that I was working on, the 'me' that I was so solidly sure of and tormented by, evaporated. What was solid and undeniable to me one moment was utterly gone in the next. I spent about three weeks in a state of unshakeable tranquility.

John: This is a beautiful pointer that shows that when the belief in the separate 'me' is questioned or seen to not be substantial, the result is that the seeking and suffering end. Those things all hinge on the assumption or belief in the 'me'. With this insight, the key is in your hands to really get to the bottom of things.

Q: During that time, chaos happened, emotions happened, events that ordinarily would have rocked me happened, and though I still felt feelings, they were small and far away, relative to the peace that reigned at that time. Serendipitously, perhaps, I found a book by 'X' (popular Satsang teacher in California) within days of that event. I also bought Nisargadatta's book 'I Am That'. I did not know 'X' existed before then, and though I had heard of Ramana and

Nisargadatta, I knew little of them. I was captured by the words in the book by 'X', because she seemed to be talking about the very thing that was happening at that time, something I did not even know was possible before. The experience of tranquility faded, actually, as I flew out to attend my first Satsang. At that point I had identified 'X' as 'the one who knew' and could deliver a verdict to me regarding what was happening.

John: At this point, you were beginning to look away from the direct experience of life outside of the 'me' construct to find some kind of confirmation or validation outside of yourself. This is fine if the pointing is truly consistent with your own clarity and understanding, but it sounds as if you were not able to get things sorted out with 'X'.

Q: A renewed sense of the insecure 'me' returned.

John: It is just that the habitual belief returned. But nothing was really lost or gained. It was just the idea of a separate 'me' floating through the clear and obvious presence that you are. The attention might have wandered onto the belief a bit because it was still believed in. So the questioning can come in to have a look and see if it is anything other than an idea without any substance. No harm at all!

Q: I felt as if I had lost something clearly seen …

John: Yes, but did you lose your presence, your awareness? The key is to realize that this is what you are and what is to be seen. It is, as I say, always shining in plain view, but we tend to overlook it and go chasing some book or teacher, as if they have the answer. But you, yourself are the answer.

Q: Over the course of the next year every book on my shelves was replaced by [long list of books by popular teachers]—I was compelled from one voice to another.

John: These are all just signposts, and some are clearer than others. Your own present true nature of being-awareness is what is to be realized. Once this is understood, all the pointers have done their job. If you look too much to the pointers, you are looking completely away from what is being pointed to.

Q: I read all of them (and I am still reading), but I feel stuck in some strange no man's land.

John: Your clear and present awareness has nothing to do with books. It is not in books. If the Self were in books, we would have realized it long ago. Just see the truth of this and come back to the looking into what is present and aware right now. Then you are immediately back on track.

Q: At this point most every belief I have seems to have dissolved, except one. Christianity was replaced by a New Age mishmash, which was replaced with a Buddhist/Hindu mélange, which was replaced by Pathwork. Now I have no beliefs left about any of them. I do not oppose them, but I cannot find an iota of conviction in myself about any of them.

John: Yes, they are just concepts, heaps of verbiage. At best, if they are clear, they point right back to the fact that what you are seeking you already are—not as a future attainment, but now.

Q: It is odd, and I feel displaced a little. I have a hard time grasping that other people still believe in various things. Yet there remains a belief in 'me' —and my investigations into that belief seem circular and at a dead end. I spin in my own confusion. I can clearly feel a sense of 'me' here. There is some unmistakable sense of existing that I take to be me.

John: There is confusion between what you truly are and what you believe yourself to be. Of course, you exist and are present. Your existence is both certain and aware, and that is what you are. Then there are all the thoughts and ideas that the mind has built up. But these are just thoughts, concepts and assumptions. You need to have a clear understanding of what you are, in order to be able to distinguish this from the ideas and beliefs in the mind.

Q: I know from last July that the 'me' I identify with now is as ephemeral as a cloud. Whatever I have been listening for in all the words I have read, I have not heard.

John: Words become a distraction. You want to understand and realize your actual nature. You are not a word. So looking in words is futile. They point to something present and existing in you that is to be known. Once you catch the drift of this, the words, the reading and the seeking are redundant.

Q: Many of the words sound a chord in me, but I am still reading, reading, reading. I get it intellectually. I am pretty sure I thoroughly get it intellectually.

John: But the real answer is not in the mind. So, basically, you are looking in the wrong direction. Just see this mistake and then you are free to see what is being pointed to. Your own being, which is all that is to be known, is not a thought, and it cannot be known in the mind.

Q: In spite of the memory of my experience last year, I do not get it at the level I intuitively seek. I turn my attention consistently to the awareness that you point to—that much

I understand now, though my mind skipped over it dismissively for a long while. But it still feels like the awareness and the 'me'—are two separate things.

John: Really look and see if you are anything apart from awareness. Is it that you are 'here' and then 'over there' there is something called 'awareness'? Just look in direct experience. If you think there is a 'me' then try to find it. Have you ever located any such entity in the picture as a 'me'? It is an assumption that we take to be present, but the key is to actually look to see what it is and if it is even present.

Dialogue on Awareness

Question: I have taken your suggestions and put down all the books, the teachers, the tapes and so on and decided to tackle this inquiry by myself. I began by clarifying my goals and decided my goal was to realize the truth. I then decided that for the truth to be true it must be consistent, ever present, never not true, self-evident and incontrovertible.

John: This is the time-tested approach recommended by many of the classical sages. If it worked for them, it will work for you!

Q: I then wrote a list of everything that could be the truth: my body, my insides, my ideas, objects outside of me, my feelings, my head, my past, the now, my standards, other people, sensations, my future and life. I then measured these things against my standard of truth and found none of them to be true. Every one of these things was changing and inconsistent. The closest item I could find to truth was the 'now', but even then if you were to ask me what it is or if it is perceivable on any level, I would say 'no'. You cannot hold it, taste it, touch it or feel it. As soon as I say 'now' it is gone. In other words, it is nonexistent—another fiction.

I then began to explore the fact that the perception of change can only be observed from the position of non-changing. But then the 'non-changing' becomes another idea, just the other end of the stick whose ends are 'changing'. and 'non-changing'. The conclusion I have arrived at is that nothing that I can perceive, conceive or experience can be the truth. This includes all teachings, books, people, places, things, ideas or experiences—present, past or future.

John: Yes, this is clearly seen. This is similar to the classic 'neti neti' or 'not this, not this' meditation suggested by the Indian sages. I would say you are on track with this. So far, so good.

Q: This leads me to awareness ...

John: Bingo. Awareness is that which is left over after everything else has been discarded.

Q: It is a puzzle.

John: To the mind it is a puzzle!

Q: It cannot be perceived, conceived or experienced at any level, but is all that is left.

John: Yes. But it is self-evident and utterly clear as that undeniable sense of 'I exist' and 'I am aware'. It is not any object, yet it is perfectly clear, present and obvious. Awareness, which is what you are, is not known objectively as something before you. It is you. It/you is present without doubt and utterly known, however. Sometimes it is called 'self-knowing' or 'self-aware'. As one teacher once said, 'Although the self cannot be known objectively, it is of all things the best known'.

Q: And also there is the puzzle of unconsciousness (as in deep, dreamless sleep) when even awareness disappears.

John: This is an assumption that may not be true. Thoughts and perceptions cease temporarily, but are you so sure that your existence and awareness disappear? Yes, objective experience stops, but are you not still present? Do you cease to exist each time you go to sleep? And the moment a thought appears, are you not there being aware of it? You need to give this some deep reflection. Thoughts are constantly arising and setting all day long. Do you disappear with the arising and setting of thoughts throughout the day? It may be that deep sleep is just another phase passing before the principle of being-awareness.

We are used to focusing on the presence of thoughts as the standard of what is happening, rather than the fact of being-awareness. Awareness may not come and go at all, contrary to our initial belief. It is good to consider whether or not thinking or reflection is the same as awareness. I would suggest they are not. Awareness knows thoughts, but it also knows the absence of thoughts.

Q: In this experiment, for awareness to be the truth it would have to be consistent, ever present, never not true, self evident and incontrovertible.

John: I would maintain that it is all of these things and more!

Q: But awareness, according to my inquiry, is discontinuous. Is this the right line of reasoning from your understanding? Any words about this break in awareness? I am having difficulty moving ahead with this roadblock.

John: It may be that it is only the objects that are discontinuous, not the awareness.

Follow up …

Q: Thank you for your response to my inquiry. Your pointers have been most helpful in assisting me with my dilemma. Yes, I can see now the detour I took by confusing thinking with awareness, and how this generated the subsequent problem of the discontinuity of awareness in dreamless sleep. The underlying assumption that the truth can only be perceived by thought, which relies on objects, is false. That which is always consistent, ever-present, never not true, self-evident and incontrovertible can never be presented by the mind because the mind has a singular flaw. That flaw is its working mechanism of polarity or duality, which makes language or thinking possible. It is almost as if language and thinking come to the edge of a cliff and cannot go any further.

John: Definitely. Seeing who/what you are is not a mental operation carried out through words. It is actually much, much simpler. We keep relying on thought out of habit, because we have been conditioned to do so.

Q: As a tool it has its limitations. For example, a screwdriver will never be a lawnmower, but a screwdriver works damn well as a screwdriver when you need it! To pursue the truth now I must abandon thinking and language because they are too small to hold it. Rather like a wheelbarrow trying to hold the universe!

John: Yes, but who says you have to pursue truth? This is still making things too complicated. You are present, you are aware. This is doubtless. And this is the truth being pointed to. You are already what you are seeking. The everyday, common and easily recognized presence-awareness is it. That is what you are and always have been. Even the urge to seek is a conditioned habit. Looking elsewhere for the truth, apart from your present awareness itself, is looking precisely away from the answer.

Q: This, unfortunately, is when things get a little weird because to jump that chasm that lies between thinking and language (the phenomenal) and the 'other' (the noumenal) is probably an act of grace.

John: Not at all. There is no chasm to jump, nor is there any entity present who needs to jump anything. You are already standing on the other shore. Present awareness is it. Full stop. It does not even need realization. There is only a pointer to a fact, not an attainment. So you can give up the search and the inquiry and just remain as you are. The answer has always been shining in plain view, but we have missed the simplicity of it.

Q: This is true especially considering that the 'other' is pre-conceptual.

John: The 'other' is what you are, even now. That in you (you!) which knows the mind now is pre-conceptual. You are non-conceptual, self-shining presence-awareness, just this and nothing else (to quote a Buddhist phrase).

Q: My current sense of this is that it is a mystery. It is very, very large, impersonal, unknowable, empty and beyond qualities.

John: It is your present, natural and easily recognized awareness. Although not an object, it is the best known of all things. Who can deny his own being, his own awareness? Look in present experience to see what you are. It is open, clear, cognizant, space-like, utterly present and utterly solid right now. It is not mysterious at all. It is so simple that we overlook it. That is the mystery—that we have overlooked the obvious for so (apparently) long.

Q: In snooping around I have seen this described as such:

> *'Having shed your skin completely, one true reality alone exists. It shines throughout all time, with no distinction of measure and time'.* Keizan

'Shining is my essential nature, and I am nothing other than that. When the world shines forth, it is only me that is shining forth'. Ashtavakra Gita

'Knowledge, what is to be known, and the knower—these three do not exist in reality. I am the spotless reality in which they appear because of ignorance'. Ashtavakra Gita

And this is where my inquiry disappears, swallowed by this enormous shining, spotless reality.

John: Well, these are all just pointers to what you are right now. You do not need books to see this which is ever-present and obvious. Remember, thou are that. And you are not in a book!

Q: There have been times in my life, John, when I sensed that looking through my eyes is this enormous presence that is absolutely still. Now I know that this is the truth. Full stop.

John: Full stop, indeed. It is what is going on right now effortlessly. It already is. No enlightenment or seeking is needed. Just do a full stop and recognize the fact of what you are—this emptiness that is nothing yet is present and brightly aware.

Q: I would appreciate your pointers and look forward to continuing this dialogue.

John: Let this strike home and no more dialogues are needed!!

38

You Are Already Free

Question: This area of what I referred to as being awake to awareness is still a bit murky, as is the idea of 'getting it' or 'losing it'. Could the confusion be something to do with the following. There is a popular teacher who says 'step out of thought and into the present moment'.

John: This is a half-step, and not that bad, but it is not precisely clear. You are present and aware now. That is what you are. There is no imaginary person to do anything. It is just a seeing of what is true. Who is to step out of thought and back to awareness? It is a subtle dualism that is not needed. If incorrectly understood, the suggestion may perpetuate the belief in a separation between 'me' and awareness. It is much more simple than this.

Q: It is clear that he places much importance on being attentive to the present moment, as opposed to being lost in worry and planning and so on.

John: It is better to see that awareness, which is what you are, is already free and not entangled in thought. There is no one to be lost, because the imagined being is not present. Rather than relying on these techniques, it is more effective to look for the presumed separate one. When you find it absent, then all the dualisms created in thought collapse and no techniques are needed.

Q: Well, that type of teaching seems to echo the Buddhist teaching of mindfulness, where it is important to be attentive to all aspects of daily activities. I suspect that many people have subliminally digested this idea of being conscious of the present moment and believe this to be what is referred to as 'awareness'. This may be why many report that they have 'lost it' and so on. Is it correct to say that your pointers differ in that you seem to be saying that moments of mindfulness and moments of forgetfulness are both just states and as states they come and go, but there is something subtly aware of all states?

John: Yes. You! Whether mindful or not, present with the 'now' or not, you remain. That 'you' is to be recognized. There is no need to be looking at the mind and its states. It is looking in the wrong direction. If you want to see the sun, you do not look at the clouds, you look at the sun. All these practices have you looking in pretty much the wrong direction, as I see it.

39

It Is All About Understanding, Not Doing

Question: My question is, how can I stop identifying with my physical sensations and thoughts?

John: You cannot do this as an act of will. There is no entity to do this anyway. This only creates a dualism. It is more a matter of understanding. Do not try to stop identifying. It is better to investigate whether or not the identity is true. When the truth is seen, the dis-identification happens by default. It is all about understanding, not doing something.

Are you your thoughts? Are you passing physical sensations? There may be an assumption that you are, but is it really true? If you are a thought, which one? If you are an emotion, which one? If you are a sensation, which one? If you are a thought, then how can you be an emotion or sensation, and vice versa. Probe into this and see what you come up with.

Q: I suppose I am not showing progress.

John: Fortunately, there is no progress and no one who can progress, so you have not fallen behind!

Q: It is very hard to explain why it is a stumbling block. But all my life I have identified with this body and these physical sensations, and the identification persists. I have to confess that I think I am a body. That thought stays. It is there so much of the time in all the focus on the physical sensations and trying to make them better.

John: Well, this is one of those acquired ideas that we picked up. It needs to be investigated. It is at the root of so many of our problems.

40

From This Seeing, Anything Can and Will Arise

Question: I have been touched by the dialogues in your book. How you expose the ordinary beliefs that keep distracting one from the truth is uncanny and uncompromising. I could never express how grateful I am to know you. Seeing the falseness of the 'me' is freedom beyond my wildest dreams. You express it so simply. Please, do not take my sense of humor and cynical personality as any lessening of my appreciation for what you have done for us. I cannot understand why certain people do not see your simple pointing to the truth as those of us who take your invitation do.

I will sneak in a question if you do not mind. With the recent tragedies in New Orleans, and the exposure of the incompetence and possible sinister intentions of the political leaders, extreme feelings and ideas arise constantly. I really do not want to block or not experience these sentiments. Can these feelings arise out of a deep compassion and not be totally revolving around the 'me'? Of course, they arise spontaneously, but sometimes the thought that I should not feel so extreme also arises. I guess I really enjoy my outrageous mind, or at least the thoughts that come. Do you have any advice? Is the play just a play?

John: The main thing is to see your real nature and the falseness of the assumed 'me'. That is the essence. From this seeing, anything can and will arise in response to the moment. It is all just a spontaneously arising movement in the appearance. Are you choosing the thoughts anyway? You can see if any of the thoughts are generating fear, doubt, suffering based on the belief in a separate 'me'. They are not necessarily doing so. There is no fixed standard as to any particular thought or experience being, a priori, self-centered. It is more in what the mind does with it. If it is not referencing any imagined defective self, then it is just something passing through. It may be a relatively clear, unclear, useful or non-useful thought in terms of the appearance, but it is not anything that knocks you out of the recognition of what is clear and present in you. So, there is no need to worry. The key is seeing that even the dreaded self-centered thought is still just a movement in the ever-clear and present being-awareness that you are. It is so incredibly simple really, but not everyone stops to notice it.

It is so simple. The truth is that you are completely, totally free and 'enlightened' even now. But you always have been, so the term 'enlightenment' is useless because it implies some sort of attainment. This is why I say 'the natural state'. It rings truer in terms of what is being pointed to.

41

It Is Just a Simple Recognition

Question: Reading your articles and listening to your interview I can relate to what you are pointing to, having had some transcendent experiences of oneness.

John: Remember, your own being-awareness is the only oneness there is. It is not transcendent at all but thoroughly present in the here and now and fully grounded in the immediacy of normal, everyday experience.

Q: This background presence, which cannot be spoken of directly but can only be known as simplicity itself, is all so familiar while reading certain words or listening to them being expressed.

John: I would encourage you to get away from the need or dependence on pointers and get back to noticing the obvious existence of presence-awareness shining in your experience at all times. It is so obvious and evident that we overlook it, because we are looking for something exotic. It is everyday, ordinary awareness.

Q: As this knowing seems to come and go ....

John: Seemingly. But your being is constantly present and solid like a rock. There is no wavering in it at all. Just get clear on what is being pointed to. We may get hung up because we are not quite appreciating what is being pointed to.

Q: Frustration arises.

John: This is a result of imagining that what is being pointed to is something difficult or hard to see. There is nothing to be frustrated about, because your being is fully clear and accessible always. We are not looking for some unusual state, but something that is present and shining in plain view all the time.

Q: There is also the understanding that nothing can be done from an individual point of view as this is somehow the wrong end to be doing from.

John: There is really nothing to be done, just a simple noticing of something we may have overlooked. It is not really a task or accomplishment, but just a simple recognition.

Q: The background needs to come forward or the foreground eliminated.

John: Not at all! This is a misconception. Awareness is shining in plain view. There is no project to be undertaken. It is much simpler than that! Just get to the heart of what is being pointed to. It is a recognition or seeing, not a project that needs to be undertaken.

Q: Is the seeing or knowing a consistent experience?

John: Your natural being of existence-awareness is effortlessly and always present. It is not an experience. It is the substratum on which all experiences come and go.

Q: Intellectually, I can know that all is an expression of oneness but...

John: Forget the 'intellectually'! Just relax with the fact of simple being-awareness that is right with you all the time and is what you are. Keep it simple!

42

What About Mundane Problems?

Question: I am an avid reader of your website. And, unless memory fails, most of the questions you publish deal with spiritual matters, for example, the seeking of enlightenment.

John: What!? As you may have come to know by now, I do not talk about enlightenment or awakening. I view this as a total concept that is confusing immense numbers of seekers.

Q: Your answers always drive home that suffering is based on the erroneous idea that we are individual, limited 'people'. You are always telling the questioner to 1) see if such an entity can be found, and 2) notice that all that can ever be found is the undeniable presence of awareness.

John: This is a fair statement. This is going right to the root of the issue.

Q: My question is about so-called mundane problems.

John: I would quibble with the wording here. Of course, with the notion of separation in play, there can arise a lot of conflict and psychological distress. This is because the view is totally out of sync with the facts. But without that notion in play, I would be disinclined to label events as problems. The word 'problems' is fairly subjective. Things are coming up to be responded to, and the body and mind do so to the best of their ability. Where does the notion of problems come into the picture?

Q: How is your teaching applied to such things, whatever we call them?

John: Relatively speaking, the body and mind just respond or not, based on their capacities or lack thereof. To speak even more relatively, I would just say to use common sense and do what is appropriate. If guidance, support or assistance is needed, then seek it. That seems like the natural, intelligent thing to do. This approach is more about resolving the core metaphysical suffering born out of a misunderstanding of who we are. It is not a prescription for how to respond to various life situations, as there are all kinds of methods and approaches available at that level. However, with the core issue of identity resolved, there are few real problems, and whatever comes up is usually dealt with without a lot of difficultly.

Q: I know 'Sailor' Bob Adamson says that nothing is wrong with right now unless we think about it. And I see that as absolutely true.

John: Good!

Q: But even knowing that, tormenting thoughts still continue to arise from time to time.

John: Based on what? Are you talking about self-centered thoughts based on the belief in the reality of a separate self? This kind of thing really drops out of the way when the core notion of the separate self is exposed. Even if any such thing arises, there is very little sting. You do not identify with/as a passing thought based on a separate self that is not there.

Q: I look and I see that there is no 'me' here actually having these thoughts, no 'me' actually having a problem. But, still, troublesome thoughts are there, along with the desire to be free of such discomfort. I see it is not 'my' desire, but desire and suffering is there nonetheless.

John: It may be that there is still some residual belief in the 'I' thought, and it is not fully exposed. There is a cause/effect relationship between the belief in the 'I' thought and the subsequent rise of self-centered thinking. I would suggest to revisit what is being pointed out as the non-existence of your identity as a separate person and see that that is really understood in the spirit intended.

Q: While it is true that nothing is wrong unless you think about it ...

John: Full stop!

Q: ... sometimes the thinking ...

John: Uh-oh! Back into thought!

Q: ... about a situation that the mind labels as problematic and distressing ...

John: Why is the mind labeling it such? Through this process, the mind lands itself in dualism. Seeing with intelligence what the mind is doing—that is, tying itself into knots—the perspective shifts and there is less inclination to give this any weight. What is, is. What happens, happens. Without labeling it, there is no real problem. Even if there is labeling, to see it as labeling also uproots the problem.

Q: But this just goes on and on, day after day.

John: Mainly because there may be some residual belief that the labels are valid and true and that our happiness is riding on all this. Once this is seen as false, the steam goes out of all this.

Q: It seems that a decision is called for, yet all choices seem to have tremendous downsides?

John: This is only when the mind under the sway of limitation gets into the picture and mucks up the works. Who cares what happens, ultimately? The body mind will eventually do something! No matter what happens you do not leave your being, the source of your peace and happiness, anyway! The belief that events contribute to our happiness may be at work here, causing the mind to worry about what happens.

Q: I am quite clear that I can find no decider, no 'decision-making process', no actual choices, except in the mind. Still, the mental turmoil does occur.

John: This pretty much drops out of the picture when you get to the root of things, so there must be something not quite clear in what is being understood. The mind is just some passing thoughts. Your being is constant and unchanging. Whatever happens or not is fairly irrelevant to who you are and your happiness. It is hard to imagine much turmoil arising with this understanding. It is just a bunch of passing events in the ever-clear presence-awareness that you are. There is likely some slight identification or investment in the thoughts and appearances.

Q: So what advice, if any, can you offer as to how to deal with distressing life situations? I know it is only conceptual to divide the mundane and spiritual, but it seems that there is a big difference between seeking enlightenment …

John: This is a total concept! Seeking enlightenment? You must not be catching the full drift of what I am communicating.

Q: What about deeper states of awareness and so on?

John: What!? You surely have missed something basic. There are no deeper states of awareness. Awareness is. Full stop. Who said anything about deeper states?

Q: Well, what about dealing with one's messy marital problems?

John: First get clear, really clear, on who you are and truly resolve the root cause of suffering. From there, most of the issues are resolved effortlessly. Almost all problems are based on our wrong belief in ourselves as a limited entity. From there you deal with things in a common sense, intelligent way based on your capacities and abilities. If you need marriage counseling, get it!

Q: Well, how do you deal with those messy marital problems or any other so-called mundane and distressing issues? No, I am not trying to turn your website into a non-dual Dear Abby!

John: Like I said, clear up the basics and you find little left over. Whatever is arising can be responded to pretty easily. Your comments and experiences lead me to believe you may not have all the basics 100% in clear view—even though you think you do! No problem! Distressing thoughts? Turmoil? Messy problems? For whom? These are self-centered thoughts based on a surviving belief in the existence of a limited, separate person and our identity with that.

If nothing else, they are only thoughts passing through the clear sky of presence-awareness. Does the sun need to do anything with the clouds? Why do you, as presence-awareness, need to do anything with mere passing thoughts? Who has determined that there is anything wrong that needs to change? That is just another self-centered thought or reference point!

43

The Sense of 'My' Vanishes

Question: This is my first 'Dear John' letter. The simplicity and gratitude of this is so overwhelming. You cut to the chase and eliminate the chaser and 'chase-ee'. No words can express this, and gratitude falls short. Besides, who is there to be grateful?

John: I am happy to provide a few pointers along the way. I am glad to hear everything is resonating so clearly for you. This is striking home. So enjoy the freedom and no-thingness that you are.

Q: I notice that along with the freedom comes a sense of something like hopelessness or indifference for 'my life'. I mean about things like money and health, especially, which are losing battles in my life story. Sometimes, there seems to be a perceptible freedom from these things. Other times, they are seen as an emotional experience, along with a sense of indifference.

John: The key—and only real import of all this—is that the sense of 'my' vanishes. It utterly vanishes. The association of experiences, feelings, events, thoughts and so on to 'me' is completely erased. Those all go on, but the association with them as belonging to me goes. Why? If there is no entity present, then who can claim them? Life goes on as before but the reference of things to a self-center, and more accurately, the belief in the reality of a self-center snaps.

There is no one left to take claim. Life cannot even be called 'mine'. It is just the appearance, the spontaneous appearance, unfolding in ever-clear, undeniable awareness-presence, which you are. Awareness has no problems. You are awareness, so you have no problems. If any of the above is unclear, make sure to verify it for yourself.

Seeing this, you can let it all end! No questions, no doubts, no problems. This is the state you are in right now.

Q: Thank you! That was the most direct answer. Freedom is so immediate and undeniable. The mind comes up with doubts as to whether or not this understanding will remain. The experience is profound. They both seem to be nothing. You are so direct. It is wonderful!

John: I had the same doubts at one point. But what are the doubts appearing in? The ever-clear awareness that you cannot shake. Basically, you can throw in the towel. When you see this for yourself, you cannot lose it. It is all about discovering what you already are. You cannot lose your own being, try as you might! So, there may be a few habitual thoughts coming up. The only thing that ever hung us up was thoughts. They rise and set right in the presence of awareness that you are. It is that simple.

Self-centered thoughts are based on a self that was never there. Once you see this, you are finished. Then kick back and enjoy the show. But there is no one there to even do that. There is just what is, as it is. The seeking is done. It is nice to see that fall out of the picture. You do not need anyone or anything. All they can do is confirm what you already know. Graduation from the school of spiritual seeking happens. Amazing, but true. It just does.

Q: Wow! These e-mails are like an arrow coming out of the computer. The experience is like a hole being blown through my reality. I am unlimited and nothing. The thoughts just keep coming with no interest. Any thinker is just another thought! Wow!

I read in your book how it is enough to see all as just thoughts. One of the thoughts is that this can be lost, especially amidst the thoughts related to body identification like fear of sickness, poverty, old age. But none of these thoughts can be true or say anything.

How much gratitude can come? I am sure you understand the sense of an incredible drawing to this freedom. Nothing matters. I cannot seem to say it coherently in words. You have pointed me to my true nature. This is the simple truth: nothing added, nothing denied.

44

Desire Is Not the Problem

Question: I wrote to you recently about how your website mainly addresses 'spiritual' subjects like enlightenment, deeper levels of awareness and so on. I only meant that that is what most, if not all, of the questions are about. I think you misunderstood me to be saying that you were about them too. On the contrary, I am quite clear that you consistently, relentlessly, unequivocally and effectively debunk them all at the very root.

But that misunderstanding notwithstanding (that is a lot of standing), you are absolutely right on target as to what my real problem is regarding the seemingly messy life situations I mentioned. You are so right about it, because whenever there does happen to be some experiencing of emotional turmoil, stress or other so-called negative feelings or states, it is absolutely incredibly effective just to see that it is all based upon the belief in a separate 'me' over here. For when there is that looking and seeing that no one can be found here to which any of this is happening, the turmoil does subside, and the frequency with which upsets arise also diminishes. So frequency, duration and magnitude of distress definitely seem to have diminished, and continue to do so, ever since the application of pointers such as yours.

Yes, I am clear that what is needed is to just keep on looking and seeing of what is always present (consciousness, presence-awareness) and the seeing of what is never present (a distinct 'me' entity), and all problems are dismantled.

It is also clear that there is a still a belief that externals can influence the quality of my life, and again, the solution is obviously the same—repeated looking to see that there is no one here to be influenced. It is all an elaborate but convincing hoax that has to be stared down by repeatedly seeing if the foundation of such beliefs is in any way real. At times this is a big challenge. But it is always rewarding, usually interesting and sometimes even fun.

You ask, where does the notion of 'problem' even come in? Perhaps I should say that there are situations, some of which seem to require a response from the mind/body organism, and it is usually no big deal.

John: What I find is that most of the issues and problems, even at relative levels, do get largely resolved through the application of the basic pointers—to the point where the following basics are clear. What is my true nature? Is the imagined separate identity which the mind has fabricated through ignorance, and all the self-concepts built on that, able to stand up to a direct investigation? With these issues fully clear, most of the problems and issues simply either disappear or else are seen in a perspective which renders them fairly inconsequential or easily dealt with. If there are any remaining issues with the body, mind or world, you find you deal with them with greater clarity and detachment and the natural intelligence within you leads you to what can be done under the circumstances. One thing is clear. You are not responding to the situation from the position of a limited, defective self, and your happiness and identity is not riding on the outcome. So there is much greater ease and sense of flexibility in response.

Q: There is clarity here that what you are saying is correct. Without the fictitious 'me' entity to which something can happen (good or bad), things are much calmer than ever. As there is relentless application over here of the pointers. There is also the direct, immediate and relatively continuous verification of what you are saying.

John: Yes. Just get to the bottom of it once and for all and then be done with the pointers!

Q: I see suffering as having two necessary components. The first is this supposed 'me' entity.

John: Yes.

Q: The other is the element of desire.

John: This takes care of itself if the first is resolved. There is nothing wrong with desire. It is a natural function, and you cannot stop it. The only problem is when it gets appropriated by the 'me' sense and the self-centered thinking. I would caution against turning desire into an enemy. It is just an impersonal function like the wind and rain. Just do not claim it on behalf of the false 'I'.

Q: When either one of these elements is seen as false, the suffering disintegrates.

John: Desire is not false per se, so I would not tackle the issue at that level. The false 'me' is definitely false.

Q: When both are seen as false, the suffering has absolutely no legs to stand on and disintegrates that much faster.

John: I never deal with desire as a separate issue. But that is just my approach. Yes, desires can be based on false assumptions, but the desire itself is just an impersonal energy, neither good nor bad.

Q: I think the main problem for me now is not in the seeing of the non-existence of the 'me' entity, nor in the direct, immediate awareness of my identity as unqualified awareness itself, but in the desire part of suffering.

John: I think you may be unclear here, but I am not sure what you are getting at.

Q: It still seems real that having a cool drink when there is thirst provides a pleasurable sensation.

John: Yes, all very fine.

Q: And having a paycheck so I can go out to a nice restaurant provides pleasure.

John: Yes, very good!

Q: And in the same way, scoring with that foxy babe over there would provide pleasure.

John: Not a problem!

Q: Based on a memory of distorted past experience (meaning, while there was some pleasure, some satisfaction in the past during such activities), there also was a great deal of pain both before and after. Yet, even though I know this, this still seems to be my Achilles heel, my weak point in dealing with suffering, because the fantasy of extreme pleasure seems nonetheless so real.

John: Pleasure is real enough as far as it goes. It is just another passing experience. If you get into fighting it you will end up in a mental struggle. Just see it for what it is. Enjoy it if you like. But it certainly will not bring in self-knowledge. It is only the thinking mind that overlays its concepts that is the issue, not the desires themselves.

Q: Then I come back to the sobering fact that since there is no 'me' entity, I cannot do anything anyway to realize my desires, so the grip of the desire lessens and a relaxation does occur.

John: You will see that it is not the desire that is the problem, but the self-centered thinking that the mind is generating and then overlaying on the desires. So get to the root of what the self-centered thinking is about and resolve that. See that clearly.

Q: But, can you provide any pointers regarding the desire element? Where is the fallacy in thinking that in the same way that a cool drink can give me pleasure when I am thirsty, a hot chick can give me pleasure when I want that?

John: There is no problem with any of it.

Q: Well, the first is usually easy, and the latter much more problematic!

John: Usually the self-centered thinking kicks in a bit more heavily!

Q: In my present experience, I do not have much of a love life and have been completely unable to find anyone with whom there is mutual attraction, interest and availability.

John: Well, you may need to go out and get some practice at dating! When you realize who you are, you may find yourself irresistible to members of the opposite sex, depending on your orientation! Why? Because you are not suffering and there is that natural self-confidence there.

Keep looking at the basics. I think the route of struggling with desires is something of a detour. But your mileage may vary.

Follow up ...

Q: Again, you are so spot on! I had definitely detoured from, or at least watered down, the clear seeing that you point to. Yes, your words are so refreshingly simple and immediately obvious as soon as they are read.

Right, I had been making desire into a bad guy, when actually it simply arises like anything else, and is not an enemy at all. It really all does just come down to continuing to notice the absence of the separate me, and the presence of awareness. It is like magic—suffering abates. It is the end of story!

John: Keep up the looking to notice your already perfect freedom and the absence of any entity in the picture at all. With no one or no thing there, who has a problem? With your identity already as that ever-fresh, ever-clear presence-awareness, who has a problem?

Stay in touch, and let me know how you do with all this.

Q: It is going great now, John! Thanks for the steadfast pointing to the simplicity. 'What is' seems to be having a pretty jolly time of it, without me there at all. One wonders how it manages without me!

John: Right, just as it always has! To imagine otherwise is/was the only problem.

Q: Just kidding. Thank you so much. Words cannot express the appreciation!

45

This Is Not a Development Process

Question: I am reading your book and really enjoying it. There are many references to 'thinking' and 'thought' in all of the books by various enlightened teachers.

John: As you may know from my book and website, I thoroughly discourage the whole concept of enlightened teachers. There are not any! There is just a truth that is being pointed to—and that truth is your true nature. All talk of enlightened teachers is thoroughly misleading. It is one of the factors that keeps seekers endlessly seeking for something they believe is missing.

Q: In my experience, many people do not have the ability to observe the process of thought. In other words, they do not know when a thought is even being experienced.

John: I am not sure about this. I think it is a pretty basic thing. Although, I agree that for most of us the conditioned attitudes and views have become so habitual that we do not realize we are viewing through the various concepts and assumptions. In that sense, I would agree with you.

Q: This allows the ego mind to hijack their experience outside their awareness.

John: It is just a process that goes on almost unnoticed until it is brought to our attention. What you are describing is not unusual. We all suffer from our thoughts and assumptions until they are questioned. That is what this is all about. By the way, there is nothing going on outside our awareness. And there is no ego mind! That is just a way of talking, but do not take it too seriously.

Q: And yet they come away from meetings or reading books with these new concepts and no direct experience of what it is like to actually see the mind delivering a thought to awareness. I hope this makes sense.

My question is, is it necessary to develop an observer or witness state as separate from thought in order to understand that awareness is right behind the 'observer' or 'witness'?

John: No. This is not about a development process, which would be yet another mental technique. It is more a pointing out of the facts, which are to be seen, not turned into a technique.

Q: I have been training my clients and workshop attendees to watch their thoughts, be the watcher, and they are all having very powerful perceptual awakenings. Many even enter the bliss for a period of time. Now when I talk about presence-awareness they know exactly what I mean. Can you comment on the value if any of this?

John: If you are established in the recognition of your natural state, then you can share what you know and what you are. I would caution against turning this into a therapeutic technique. That is fine as far as it goes, but you have to be aware about passing along some of your own misunderstandings.

This is not about perceptual shifts or bliss experiences, far from it. Those are still just transitory states and of no real lasting benefit. Basically, people cycle back to the old beliefs and patterns until the whole process is clearly laid out and understood.

This demands a high degree of interest and commitment to self-knowledge based on a deep desire for freedom and interest in the subject. It cannot be doled out as a matter of course as a workshop technique. Like Nisargadatta Maharaj used to say, you cannot put anyone else beyond the need of further help until you are beyond help yourself.

There is one issue on the table. Have you seen the truth of what is being pointed out for yourself? If you have, you do not need my help because you will know the fundamentals. So, look into yourself and see if there are any remaining doubts and questions in your personal experience.

Follow up ...

Q: I am honored by your reply. I guess my point is summed up best by you—'Awareness knows thoughts, but thoughts can never know awareness'.

I am simply encouraging the experience of awareness knowing thought. It is not a technique. It is a knowing, a noticing. I find that this basic thing is overlooked. When this happens, the mind tries to mimic awareness. Then the person is hopelessly lost in thinking that they get it. But, you are right. There are no doubts, but it is not solid yet.

John: Awareness is not a technique or even a noticing. It is simply a fact that is pointed out—and there is not much to be done with it! The fact is that whatever you think, say, or do, awareness must be there as the background for any of that to occur. And that is what you are. Whether the mind is engaged in noticing or not does not change the simple fact.

The other thing is that there is no entity present to get it or not get it. There can be a recognition of your identity as that presence-awareness and the understanding that there is a complete absence of any individual entity in the picture. Then the seeking and suffering, practicing and techniques, noticing and not noticing are over. One does not really approach this as a methodical, step-by-step process or technique. Why? Who would be doing such a thing? Only the imagined separate one who thinks he is present and needs to do something!

If you can say anything about it, perhaps you can say it is a radical paradigm shift. But nothing really changes. We were living under a misapprehension, a mistaken belief. That gets exposed through inquiry and drops away. But still you are what you have always been.

All thinking within time, techniques, approaches and so on are still within the old paradigm. Most of what is passing for spiritual teachings and even non-dualistic meditation is actually operating within the paradigm of separation and belief in a separate entity. As such, it continues to re-enforce the root misunderstanding.

46

Getting Along with Others

Question: I am reading your book and it is very clear and helpful. My question with this teaching is that we still live our life on earth with others. Some are not very nice. Can you say something about getting along with others?

John: 'Self', 'others', 'nice' and 'not nice' are mental ideas or labels put on by the mind. Viewing the world through these labels is where the division comes in. Without the labels, you see things more completely, more holistically. The root of all labels, and the source of all suffering, is the 'I' label. Once that kicks in and is believed, then there are 'others' apart from me. Then there is division, strife and discord. Without that 'I' belief, you do not view yourself as separate from anyone or anything. It is all one movement, one expression of life. And things come up to be done according to circumstances. There is no sense of loss or gain, because you are free of division and always remain in your wholeness. It does not mean that there are not challenges or undesirable things, but you see them from a more objective viewpoint. You do what you can, if you can help. You just respond naturally, knowing that ultimately everything is, in each moment, just as it must be.

47

The Real You

Question: What is the separate individual? How can I look for it if I do not know what I am looking for? It seems impossible to get started without defining our terms, right? So, am I looking for an entity which needs no world or universe to live in or for an object which contains me, my being-awareness? I think the latter is closest to what is meant. However, it is a contradiction in terms, an anomaly. Awareness is not an object, so how can it be contained therein? At this point, the pointers lose coherence. You cannot point at something which has neither location nor substance. I am not putting down the pointers. I am just saying they cannot be used on the apparent terms in which they are stated.

John: You are somewhat jumbling up the being-awareness aspect and the separate individual. What you are is simple presence, which is existent and aware. It is simple and needs no particular investigation. Do not turn it into a quest, which is just a mental activity that comes in due to not seeing how simple this is. It is so simple that there is nothing to do. You are present and aware. That awareness shines continuously and is that space in which the body, mind and world arise. That is the real you. If you 'try' to get it, you will immediately make it an object and some kind of attainment and go off searching for something you think you do not have. Those thoughts are the only disturbance. And they are based on a misperception. See how silly this is. You are that.

Awareness (you) has no problems at all. It is untouched by the mind and world, just the like the sun always shining above the clouds. It cannot be sought. It is. When you begin to speak from the perspective of a limited, problematic someone, then the notion of a separate, limited self comes in at the mental level. We say:

- I am not happy.
- I am not there.
- I do not like this.
- Why are they doing that to me?
- And so on.

The 'I' and 'me' in those statements is what I am calling the separate self. It is a verbal construction, an image, an idea. So, when you say 'I am no good' or whatever, the question is: What is that 'I'? It certainly is not the pure being-awareness, which is the eternal and perfect reality itself, is it? Then what is it?

This is the inquiry being suggested, if you are drawn to it. We are constantly saying 'I', 'me', and so on. So who and what is this 'I'? That is the question. It is a very precise and clear question and there is nothing fuzzy about it. Are you a body? Are you the mind? Are you a thought? Are you an emotion? Look at these questions and answer them. If you are a thought, which one? If you are a feeling, which one? If you are none of those things, then who are you?

What you discover is that you cannot find any particular thing or experience that is 'I'? There is nothing present that is the limited, separate self. It is just a notion, but does not exist in fact. We are talking about a phantom that is not present. It is an assumption. Yet, we undoubtedly are. What are we truly? As I started with—we are that undeniable presence-awareness that is always here. It is clear, simple and free of problems.

This looking dissolves the habitual belief we have of taking ourselves to be a small, limited, defective person. That assumption survives because we hold to that belief. Look at what you truly are or discard what you are not. It all comes back to the same thing in the end—the recognition of what you are and always have been.

My advice is to drop the attitude of trying to find an experience or get free. This is a thought that is based on a misunderstanding. You will really take off with this when you begin to question 'Who needs to get free?' 'Who am I?' 'What is my nature?' 'Am I really bound?' Then you will step off the mental track and stop taking a ride with the conceptual mind when it tosses up its old beliefs.

You are not a limited being in need of anything. You are that, the ultimate reality itself.

48

See the Basics for Yourself

Question: When I work with my clients and workshop attendees, I 'point out' that there are thoughts occurring and urge them to look, become aware, notice mind activity. This takes several weeks. What happens in the end is the person begins to have the moment-by-moment experience of thought. In the process, they learn to avoid the temptation to identify with thought, to enter into the drama, or the story. Finally, there is an understanding that they are not thought. They are not even the thinker.

This is usually accompanied by an epiphany, insight, awareness, breakthrough, awakening, whatever term is appropriate for a paradigm shift. Many report being able to 'see through the eyes of God', watching the watcher and many other descriptions. At this point, they see clearly their motives, issues and perceptual distortions and they can see the same in those around them.

I call this the 'witness consciousness'. And by the way, this is not done during mediation. It is done each moment that the person remembers to do it. Eventually there is a state of detachment that is entered that is palpable. Maybe it is not a step, process or whatever. Now they can come to your workshop or read your book and they intuitively know and resonate with what you are saying.

John: What I mainly do is work one on one directly with folks. My only question is whether or not YOU have any question or doubts about any of this. Once you see this for yourself, you can easily share your experiences with whomever you work with and the kinds of questions you have asked would not arise with any particular force, because you would know the answers from first-hand experience.

To talk too much about what other people are getting or not or what their issues might be with understanding is not that relevant in my book. So my preference is to dialogue directly with you about your understanding. I would shy away from using this as a therapeutic technique to be applied en masse. I would encourage you to look into your heart and see if there are any remaining doubts and questions. If not, then you are on your way and you do not need me. If there are some questions, then let us have a dialogue—you and me. You need to climb into the test tube yourself.

There is another subtle point to this. Too much talk about 'others' is moving away from the heart of the matter, because the very notions of 'self' and 'others' are going to be dissolved. So there is no need to put much weight on the concept.

Q: Yes, I see the wisdom entirely in what you are saying. I am nearly finished with your book, and I find your message the most powerful and straightforward yet. Reading it has removed any doubts. But I do need you.

John: If your doubts are gone, you most assuredly do not need me! There is no need to assert any understanding or lack thereof. Just make sure you see the basics for yourself. Often people want to push for some statement that 'they have it' (whatever it is!), which is not useful at all.

Q: I am looking forward to being in your presence

John: If you still think you need me, then you have not completely seen the basics. No harm. I will just point back to what is already present in you. Keep in mind there is nothing particularly interesting about my 'presence'. This is all basic and natural stuff available to anyone at all times. Do not build it up into some glorious concept.

Q: The sense of presence-awareness is, as you describe it, subtle. I want to be captured by it.

John: Let the sense of 'I' disappear through investigation. Then there is no one left who needs to be captured. As long as there is a belief that 'I' exist as something apart from presence-awareness, you are a slave to that thought. Liberation, if there is any such thing, is the discovery that you have never been in bondage.

Who Is Aware of the Thought 'I'?

Question: You replied to a questioner that if they had been around all this for more than a few months and still were not getting it that they were overlooking something and should enter dialogue. Well, I have tried dialogue and it has not worked. There still seems to be a solid, independent, separate self here.

John: Well, keep it simple. What do you suppose is the solid, independent self? If there is one you should be able to find it. What have you come up with?

Q: I cannot look to see if there really is one because it seems like it is the separate self who is doing the looking.

John: No, not at all. That is just an assumption. It is just a natural looking. Do not block yourself by getting too sophisticated with all this. This is the mind hijacking the investigation and fishing for delaying tactics.

Q: Other thoughts can be seen as just thought but not the 'I' thought.

John: The thought 'I' is just another thought. But who is aware of the thought 'I'?

Q: When I am told to investigate the 'I' and see if there is one, I do not know how an 'I' could investigate itself.

John: Again, do not get too mental. It is not an 'I' that is looking, it is you who are looking. Just go ahead and look and see if there is tangible, conceivable thing present that you can sense, observe or know that you are willing to call yourself. Are you a thought, an emotion, a sensation? What particular thing are you?

Q: Yes, awareness is present, but it seems to be a separate 'I' who is aware.

John: This is the crucial misunderstanding—to differentiate yourself from awareness. You are awareness itself. Is that a separate entity, an individual? Everything, including the world, arises and sets in the one awareness that you are. That is not a limited individual at all. It is completely devoid of any individual at all. That is what you truly are. To imagine yourself as some independent, isolated entity apart from awareness is the crucial error. Looking for that separate self, you cannot find it at all, and your identity returns to that natural, effortless awareness that you are and always have been.

Q: Thank you for your reply. I have had several phone conversations with a particular teacher about all this. He emphasizes that it is 'seeking' for our true nature that is stopping us being able to be simply present.

John: Everyone has a different way of talking about things. You do not need to seek for your true nature, because it is what you are. Just notice what is being pointed to—the simple fact of present being-awareness. It is so clear and present that we overlook it. In the end you give up all the pointers. You are what you are. It takes no pointers to be.

Q: The assumption that there is somebody here seems to be set in stone.

John: It is just an idea. All there is, is simple undeniable presence-awareness. There may be a few thoughts, emotions or sensations passing through, never anything else. There is absolutely nothing substantial in the picture at all. If you think there is a person there, then try to point out exactly what and where that is.

Q: I told you in an email about a year ago that I had looked within when I was very young and seen for a moment that there was nobody here but awareness. So I know that what you are saying is true.

John: There is no need to go to the past. It is clear and present now.

Q: To look now seems to be the hardest thing. As you say, I am making it mental.

John: Just let the simple pointers strike home.

Q: Are there other ways than 'looking to see if there is anyone' for awareness to recognize itself and stop taking itself to be the character?

John: Just see it is only thoughts arising and setting in the clear, boundless and bright awareness that you are. It is that simple and can be done right now. There is nothing to get or understand, really, just see the simplicity of what is here. Drop the idea that there is some great attainment. What is being pointed to as what you are is plain, old, everyday awareness. It is what is looking out of your eyes right now.

50

Awakening Is a Fallacious Concept

Question: After speaking with you, I have continued to probe, as you suggested. I have no doubt of the truth of what you, 'Sailor' Bob and others keep hammering away at—that I am the present awareness, not a separate entity. I seem to get glimpses of this, just for an instant, at various times of the day.

John: It is not about glimpses! Glimpses by whom and of what? Can you deny the fact of your very existence, your very awareness at any point during the day? Is it a matter of glimpses or is it just a fact? Try to settle that. We are not looking for anything special at all, just what is here.

Q: But what you described as 'simple' is also so radically different from what we have been conditioned to believe—that I am 'this' body and 'this' mind, which is separate from everything else.

John: At least now you are starting to see all those ideas for what they are—conditioned beliefs! That is all they are, just ideas. They have not been questioned till now.

Q: It is true I cannot show you this separate self. But the belief in the separate entity is hard to shake.

John: There is no need to shake it. Who would, anyway? Present awareness does not need to shake anything. Just investigate the belief until you are convinced that it is only a belief, based on no factual evidence whatsoever. It is neither a difficult nor protracted process at all.

Q: I am wondering, how does one keep reminding one's self of this present awareness? Or is it something that just gets noticed occasionally, as I appear to be doing now, until it becomes continuous?

John: You come to realize that the resolution of all your doubts, suffering and problems are riding on the seeing of this. How much motivation does it take to drop a red-hot poker? Just understand why this is important, and there will be no lack of motivation.

Q: A second question is: Once one experiences oneself constantly as present awareness, not as a separate entity, why would one concern oneself at all with separate entity 'stuff'—mowing the lawn, washing the car, brushing the teeth?

John: This all goes on quite well and naturally, just as always. Are 'you' beating your heart? It happens intelligently and spontaneously. So do the other functions. No 'one' is doing them, as such. Yet they all happen just fine.

Q: If separate existence is illusory, why pay any attention to it at all?

John: Who are you talking about? You previously denied, at least in theory, the existence of a self, and now talk about why 'one' would or would not do something. There is a lack of consistency in this. Once the separate self is exposed as non-existent, all these questions really do not arise. They are self-centered questions based on the assumption of individuality. Can you see that?

Q: I think of someone like Ramana Maharshi, who reportedly stopped taking care of himself totally after his awakening.

(I recognize that this type of worry is probably just the mind throwing up roadblocks!)

John: Awakening is a totally fallacious concept. He just stopped one day and noticed the fact of his own being, which is the same self that you are right now. No awakening is needed. Then the body and mind just do whatever they spontaneously will do. There is no blueprint for anything.

51

The Mind Has Thoughts, Not You

Question: In your book you say that awareness is not affected by thought.

John: Yes, true.

Q: But whenever I have negative thoughts, I get bad feelings. So I am still affected by thought.

John: There is the catch. Do 'you' have bad feelings, or are there simply thoughts and feelings arising in present awareness? Does the sun 'have' rain clouds or thunder storms? It is the mind that has thoughts, not you. You are simply aware of the mind. It is like lying on the grass looking at the clouds. Do you 'have' clouds? Are they 'your' clouds? No, not at all! You do not identify with them, and they just blow through. You, as the knower of them are unaffected. So, thoughts generate more thoughts, but you are the knower of them. You are the space in which they appear and disappear. What happens to the sun when the clouds come and go? Does awareness get disturbed with the appearance of thoughts? It is there before, during and after all thoughts. That is you. Your real nature is undisturbed.

Q: How do I find that in me that is unaffected by thought?

John: Just look as I am indicating and discover that you remain as you are, regardless of whatever thoughts, feelings or sensations are passing through.

52

The Body Is a Concept

Question: I am reading your book and have finished about half of it. I notice that it generally shuts my mind up to read it and investigate as you say to do. I find interesting the ever-present awareness you talk about, what I would call the 'pilot-light awareness', which is always present irregardless of thoughts, feelings and so on. Like the ocean beneath the storms, or like the gas pilot light on an old heater, it continues shining unaffected by the various shadows thrown out onto the floors and wall by its light.

Here is one of my doubts. In our culture, as you know, they would say that what you are describing is strictly generated by the body and that when you die the pilot light is turned out permanently. To prove this they would point out that deep sleep puts it out, not to mention anesthetics you might get from, say, an oral surgeon, which totally seem to annihilate it. So, while I am very drawn to what you are saying this is my chief doubt, the doubt which all of science and western civilization lays on us from the time we start first grade.

John: The body is just a concept, a label. It does not exist, as such. 'Body' is a word for a series of arising experiences, sensations, feelings and so forth. So we are talking of a collection of events labeled with a word. Does 'San Francisco' exist, as such? Where is it, precisely? It is the same with the body.

In present experience does a sensation arise in awareness, or does awareness get generated from a sensation? The short answer is that the body appears as an object in awareness, as does the whole universe. Those things constantly arise and set but your being remains. If in doubt, check it out until you see it. Yes, it is the complete reverse of what the common view is—but look where the common view has gotten us!

53

Pure Clarity and Joy

Question: Thank you so much for the clarity that you shared last night. Since the meeting there has been an apparent going between awareness ('be-ing') and habitual contraction into the phantom identity ('me-ing') with thoughts such as 'X got it and I did not', 'John gave X attention and ignored me', 'I am not getting it', and so on. Then I would ask, 'To whom are these thoughts arising?' and look for the separate 'me'. And of course in not finding the 'me', the shift would happen. There was not much sleep during the night, and the dreams were all about presence-awareness and the questioning. It continues today. Of course, the awareness is always there. Any suggestions for working with the 'me' when it arises would be welcomed.

John: Just come back to the simple noticing that these are only thoughts arising in the ever-clear, ever-bright presence of awareness that you are. They neither touch nor diminish your true nature in anyway. Yes, question the very existence of the separate 'I', which is the foundation of all the limiting thoughts. Look at that until you are convinced that there is no such ghost in the machine. That takes the energy out of the core concept sustaining all the self-centered beliefs. The limited, problematic person has never been there. The presence of existence-awareness is here beyond any doubt. Your identity as that is clear and also beyond doubt. Who needs to get what when this is seen to be the case?

Follow up ...

Q: The seeming reality of the separate self is not sustainable any longer. The questioning has taken all the wind out of the sails of that supposed identity. Thoughts still appear and feelings are felt, but they are not really able to hook onto anything. Everything is the same yet so, so different. Thank you.

John: It is good to see that the basics have become clear for you. As you are seeing, nothing in the appearance needs to change at all. It is just that things are no longer referred to a separate self. Once that belief is investigated, it simply falls away, and the referencing of things to an assumed person fades, along with all the suffering and doubts generated by that notion. What remains is the undeniable presence of awareness that you are and always have been. It is the simple recognition of what you are, which is pure clarity and joy.

Q: Yes!

54

The Limits of Thought

Question: Since I have been looking at the ongoing 'I-me-mine' process, all kinds of things have been coming up. First of all, there are the constant protests of the mind, such as, 'All this non-dual stuff is nonsense', 'I just cannot get it', or 'I cannot seem to go deep enough to gain the clarity' and so on. But then I simply question why I should believe in what the mind is not understanding, since it only causes suffering, creates insoluble problems, and cannot really give a satisfactory answer that is free from doubt anyhow. So, consequently, all these thoughts quickly fade when they are not indulged in.

I have actually been observing all this, so there is no doubt about this. Constant questioning and doubting are really getting very boring now, especially because they are so endless if given the chance. Nevertheless, some of what you say does not seem to make sense to me yet, and I am frustrated. I still feel like a separate body which has awareness and sees everything else as separate objects. If my true nature is simple, unlimited awareness, it still seems to have certain limitations. For instance, I know that there is a tree outside my window, even if I am not directly aware of it. Reason tells me it has not walked away since I last looked at it five seconds ago. The mind seems to be a tool to 'fill in the gaps' of physical limitations.

I just do not seem to see that my true nature is 'already free of time and space and limitation'. As I am writing this, I am feeling more frustrated and realize I am doing the opposite of what I said in the first few sentences that offered at least an inkling of freedom. Help! I am addicted to thinking and philosophical speculation.

John: You will find that when we get tied up in various riddles of thought and experience, we are inevitably focusing on the objects and experiences in awareness. Then we begin puzzling over conundrums created in the mind, which is unable to explain appearances to its satisfaction. An exclusive reliance on the mind leads, even under the best circumstances, to skepticism and doubt. That is not a problem inherently, but may be frustrating if you are hoping to arrive at certainty that way. That is why there are various pointers such as 'the answer is not in the mind' and so forth.

Interestingly enough, the fact of your being-awareness is not susceptible to this kind of doubt. It is that in you which is shining 'upstream' of the mind. The world of thoughts, sensations, feelings and appearances is arising at the level of the mind. The ultimate nature of those things is really not determinable by the mind. Thinking about those things can generate more and more uncertainty. Practically, it may be more useful to focus the inquiry on the doubtless sense of being-awareness, rather than on objects. The habit has been to look at what is objective, instead of the subjective aspect. The key lies in the recognition of the subject. From there, an understanding of the objects will come in naturally. Starting with the objects is not as conclusive because doing so activates the mind as the instrument of inquiry, which has some inherent limitations, as mentioned above.

If you come back to the fact of being, which is both present and aware, everything solidifies considerably. However, if you start conceptualizing, philosophizing and debating about your nature as a topic of intellectual discussion, you touch down again into thought and are back in its limitations. That is why all this is not really about thinking about it. It is about direct, non-conceptual realization of your true nature.

There is no need to worry. You are just bumping up against the limitations of thought and seeing those limits graphically demonstrated in your experience. It is actually good to see this. This is proof-positive that the answer is not in the mind.

No One Left to Have Problems

Question: I have practiced Zen for thirty years with Japanese or European masters in Riutakudji, Tokyo, Paris and London. I have gone through some koans. But I must say that in reading some of your articles recently I have realized with clearness and an unaccustomed intensity what is meant by no-separation, egoless and emptiness. You have unearthed the inner being which is this intimate yet universal presence we are invited to contemplate and then be during Zazen meditation and afterwards. How many have been the long hours and days of meditation (and, I dare say, suffering!) until now. Your words made a real breakthrough. My first master told me, 'Kill Jim!' (my name). You can see here the typical 'brutality' of Zen! But I insist—never had the absence of 'Jim' been so clearly and easily perceived than in reading your conversations. Of course, the 'I' is yet lurking behind the door. That is why I want to ask if you could send me a word (or two) to help in this seeing of the natural state (which I presume is the same as the 'Buddha Nature', as they call it in Zen)?

John: All that I can say is that the presence of awareness which is with you right now, that simple sense of existence which is brightly aware, is your true nature. It needs no attainment because it is fully and clearly present. Awakening and enlightenment are at best concepts attempting to point to the ever-awake and clear presence that you are. Once understood, no awakening is called for. It is the recognition of your natural state, which has been present all along, but perhaps unnoticed. We search and meditate as long as we are not clear that what we are seeking we already are. What you are is not a limited entity, but the clear, knowing-presence in which all appearances rise and set. Know this and be at peace. All the imagined problems and doubts fall to pieces when you see this. There is no one left to have problems. There is only open, clear, spacious presence-awareness.

56

You Remain as the Empty Sky

John: The body and mind arise based on causes and conditions. They swirl around for a time and disappear. Some bodies and minds look one way. Others look another way. Does life have an opinion? See them for what they are—passing images in the ever-clear and doubtless awareness that you are. It is not the appearance and what it does or does not do that is really the issue. Rather, it is the exclusive identification as that, taking that to be what I am. Are you a cloud, a passing breeze, a honking car horn? Do we even care much about those things? What else are bodies and minds but passing experiences in awareness? Why should we take delivery of them and claim them as 'I' and give much thought to them at all?

Question: Last night, the inquiry 'Who am I?' woke me up and dug deeply for remaining habits of limiting thought that still arise in awareness. And so the understanding that I am consciousness is re-cognized. Energies arose in the body that the mind wanted to name. It labeled them 'fear'. Thoughts about lack, about there not being enough money coming in to meet the overhead attach themselves to the fear, and a thought-storm tries its damnedest to take over and bring about more suffering, but for who? Me? What me? What is me? Where is it? Presence just is, always here and now. Back, back, before mind, feeling, energy, emotion. That blank empty cognizing just is. All is well. It was/is clear as a bell sounding in silence.

John: Suffering, doubts, fear, problems, issues, questions and so on are simply arisings in thought. They are just passing thoughts. Apart from thought, they have no substance, no reality, no being whatsoever. How many of those things can you have without thoughts?

The body, world, other people, events are simply what they are. They are neither good nor bad. They are just arisings. They are all impersonal, and there is not a problem with any of those things. Getting all worked up about others, ourselves or our thoughts implies we are giving them way too much reality, reality which they do not warrant.

What we are always—and ever—dealing with are thoughts. Thoughts are simply stories spinning in empty space (the space of awareness). Our only issue is taking them to be true, particularly the ones that attempt to tell us who and what we are. These are the self-centered thoughts, thoughts about me. But what is this supposed 'me' they are all talking about? Have we ever found it? All the doubts and issues are for a fictional character. You, as a separate person, have never really existed except as an assumed character. If this is so, how can we take all the thoughts about him too seriously?

Seeing this, the absorption and fixation on the passing thoughts and content of the mind drops away. If there is still some absorption and fixation, then there is still some belief going into the thoughts. They are not being seen as just thoughts, but as something real and valid. This is not to deny practical issues and concerns. It is not a license to abandon common sense and the need to address practical concerns, as and when they arise.

What are self-centered thoughts? Just habits and beliefs picked up in the years of ignorance when we did not know any better. There is nothing right or wrong about them. They are just mechanical reflexes. The key is to see them for what they are. Note that the appearances of the body or mind need not change or be any different. Whatever comes up will come up, and do we choose anyway? Nor is this denying the relative appearance or devaluing it in any way.

Seeing all this, the exclusive focus can come off the content of the mind. Then there is space to recognize that true nature that you are, that clear presence of awareness shining upstream of the mind. That is what you truly are. That is not conditioned by the body-mind mechanism at all. Let the focus come off of the body-mind appearance. Forget about what others think and say about you, and you say about them. That is all a bunch of fictional characters talking in their sleep! Everything comes to balance with the clear recognition of your true nature. Knowing who you are, the body and mind are left to play out their allotted roles in the appearance.

With a bold decision, simply see all suffering, doubt and confusion as thoughts arising in the mind. Then turn to that in you which knows the mind and all else and claim that as your identity. That is the constant presence of being-awareness that remains untouched no matter what is going on in the mind. With your identity firmly rooted as that presence-awareness, the exclusive identification and abiding interest in the thoughts withers away. Experiences are left to blow in and out of your being like autumn leaves across a field. You remain as the empty sky—bright, clear, open, embracing all, yet utterly untouched by whatever passes through you.

Follow up …

Q: Can it be as simple as not believing any thought to be true? It seems so. I am continuing to be with your last message. It is opening something up.

John: Relative, practical thoughts about things and events may or may not be true, but those are not really the issue at stake here. We are talking about self-centered thoughts, thoughts about who I am, what I am, what my attributes are. Of course, we can talk about the attributes of the body and mind. But to grasp hold of those thoughts and believe they say something about me, that they are true statements of who and what I am is where the rub lies. They are all categorically false. How can the spacious, clear no-thingness of presence awareness have any mind-created labels and attributes? Is the clear sky of awareness, which is what you are, good or bad, enlightened or unenlightened, high or low? Those are all attributes of a supposed someone who we take ourselves to be.

We believe those attributes because we assume the person having them is present and is who we are. So, see those attributes and all the turmoil they generate as mere ideas, movements arising and setting in the mind, with no other substantial existence. Once they are seen as ideas, then you are in a position to question whether they are even true or not, as you are doing. The clincher is the deep recognition of why they are not true. They are not true for two reasons. One, your nature as that natural clarity of presence-awareness does not conform to any of the concepts the mind asserts you to be. To discover what you really are fundamentally undercuts all the self-centered beliefs in the mind. Two, the self-centered thoughts apply to a person or entity that, upon investigation, simply cannot be located. Finding the non localized, concrete limited self in the picture severs the root of the whole conceptual mechanism. The whole network of false ideas and limiting beliefs is seen for what it is—thoughts floating in the space of clear presence-awareness, just like a handful of dry leaves spinning through the wide open, clear autumn sky. Nothing is gained, but the true perspective is restored.

57

No Awakening Needed

Question: I will get up to Santa Cruz to one of your talks soon. Awakening has to be close. I am hoping to get a boost, maybe like when you resonated with 'Sailor' Bob Adamson on your visit to him.

John: You say 'awakening has to be close'. The notion of awakening is really just another concept—a very attractive one, no doubt! It tends to keep the mind spinning, imagining something that it does not have yet.

The knowingness that is shining in you right now, as the undeniable presence of awareness that is utterly clear and evident is all that is being pointed to. There is no awakening needed. When you see the obviousness of what is being pointed to, the concept of awakening will fall away, and you will see that what you are seeking you already are.

58

Awareness Is the Background of All Experiences

Question: Greetings from India! This note comes to you as a mark of heartfelt gratitude for your clear, unrelenting pointers. For the past few months, I have kept coming back to your site again and again. A lot of clarity has happened in the process. The resonance is unmistakable, and not mental. Thank you for that.

Very recently, the completely imaginary nature of 'I' finally kicked in, and with a little 'effortless effort' of staying with awareness rather than going with the thought train, clarity shone in full view. All remaining questions, doubts, dilemmas were seen as just random mind activity, with no real substance. And the depth of peace, security, love, and joy this clarity brings is felt to the core. Also, it is seen that awareness or the clarity is all that is. It is not a momentary arising, but that in which everything arises. And so whatever comes is seen as an appearance. This includes thoughts, feelings, old mind patterns, fears and thoughts and ideas about this whole teaching. There are moments when the mind poses questions about what is happening (since this amount of certitude and peace is very new) and some mild mind-wrestling begins. But awareness sees that as well, and the peace returns. It is seen, too, how simple it all is. It is nothing mystical, nothing spiritual, just the fact of being. I guess that is the state little babies are in before they have grown 'smart' enough to imagine themselves as separate!

However, when I go out in the midst of people (we are having a major festival these days, and there are community celebrations), I can see questions on whether I am still aware arising. Even though I have completely seen the falseness of the separate 'I', this doubt makes a return when I am among a multitude of people. Along with it, other questions arise and there is an 'effort' to remain aware and present. This brings in some confusion, even though I recognize it to be insubstantial mind activity. When I am back home, I find such questioning lessening, and there is a sort of 'return' to the basics as you point out. Can you relate to this kind of situation? I hope I made myself clear here.

It has been great reading your pointers. As I apply them more and more, I am certain of everything you say—from direct experience and not mental understanding. However, some unnecessary loose ends still seem to hang. I know, for whom? But when they do pop up, the mind just tends to become the dominant player. I would love to hear from you, if you have anything to point me to. Once again, thanks for being there, sharing your experience that obviously emanates from the headquarters of shining awareness.

John: Thanks for being in touch and sharing your insights. All sounds good. It looks like the pointers are striking home. The basics are clear for you: 1) the undeniable presence of awareness that you are, and 2) the non-existence of any substantial entity in the picture you can grasp hold of and call 'myself'. These are the core insights.

A couple of comments. The awareness that you are is effortlessly present and needs no maintenance. In fact, it is impossible to get out of that shining presence of being-awareness. It is just an undeniable and inescapable fact. All thoughts, perceptions and sensations necessitate the presence of your being-awareness to even be cognized. It is the permanent background of all experiences. Even the absence of experience must be registered on that background. You are that background. All else is just an appearance arising and setting in this that you are.

To imagine that we existed as some separate limited self apart from our nature of presence-awareness was the only problem. However, investigation reveals that there is no separate entity or self in the picture. All the other habits and identifications were based on that initial false assumption. They only survived as habits or beliefs in the mind.

They may continue to arise for a time, simply due to the fact that they are habits. Yet once this is seen, you cannot believe them with the same force as previously. They are seen as clouds passing in the ever-clear sky of awareness that you are. Nothing needs to be done. They will depart of themselves. If you find yourself troubled by them, just see that they are thoughts or habits referring to an imagined self. Then come back to see that the separate self is also just an idea—and there is no such thing. Immediate looking reveals that you have never departed from the clear awareness that you are. Seeing this, all the belief in the ideas is undercut and you simply rest as that presence that you are.

After a bit of looking like this, you simply must admit that this natural state is your ongoing position. It is not an attainment, but just a recognition of the natural state of affairs, which was always present but overlooked. All of this becomes clear easily and naturally as the basics settle in, as they are for you now. Feel free to stay in touch if you have any other questions or comments to share. I would enjoy hearing from you.

59

There Is Only Seeing

Question: I am having the impression that this awakening issue is such a simple matter.

John: Yes, especially when you drop the need for any awakening at all! That ends up being a burdensome concept when the simplicity of this is seen. Who needs to awaken, and to what, when everything is shining in plain view? Suffering, awakening, seeking, renouncing, seeing, not seeing—all are just empty words floating the obvious presence-awareness that you are. You are that. All appearances arising within it are only that. There is only that.

Q: It is the simple realization that all is fine and there is no doer named 'me'.

John: Yes, without the belief in the separate 'me' everything is just an arising and falling in each moment, and nothing is wrong anywhere.

Q: When this is realized an enormous load is lifted from one's mind.

John: Yes, and what a relief it is.

Q: Therefore, whatever arises is rightful. Whatever it is, is not 'my' doing.

John: It is all just spontaneous functioning of intelligence in each moment without reference to a self center.

Q: Awakening is the removal of all imagination about what is really occurring, isn't it?

John: It is just seeing straight out, as is, without viewing through the binding concepts of self and other, and all the other dualistic judgments and evaluations.

Q: Nothing is added. There is only seeing and humble freedom. There is no need to explain life—this fleeting and, in essence, wordless appearance on the stage of consciousness. All happens by itself, the suffering, the seeking, the world, the 'I am' and the ultimate seeing of what is.

John: Beautifully said.

Q: Fine states of mind and the psychic powers one hears about may or may not arise, and it does not matter at all. This freedom is independent of anything imaginable or desirable. The 'me' has learned to desire so many experiences and it suffers endlessly in the pursuit of their satisfaction.

John: Again, most beautifully expressed.

Q: It has been such an amazing ride from the grossest suffering to an understanding such as this and back to suffering. All this must be, so it is rightful and perfect. And I do not know what the next moment will bring, nor does it matter.

John: I would say that what is is not even rightful and perfect. It is just as it is and must be in each moment. If the mind must put a label on it, then 'rightful' and 'perfect' fill the bill.

Q: I have tried to formulate questions to ask you since our last contact but it all feels void of substance. Most concepts fade into thin air as soon as attention goes into them. It all comes back to this moment of seeing in solitude. Even if there is much pain it always comes back to this moment of seeing. The seeker seeks assurance but it cannot come from anywhere but from this looking inside, in this moment.

John: Thanks for being in touch. Nice to hear from you. The key is the simplicity of it, as you are seeing. I appreciated reading your insights and observations. The basics are settling in quite well. Your words are a clear expression coming from your own direct knowing.

60

Awareness, Sleep and Suffering

Question: I heard your interview with Allin Taylor and wanted to ask you a question about sleep. If we are present awareness, as consciousness, then what happens to us during dreamless sleep? It seems to me that we are neither conscious nor aware during dreamless sleep. I appreciate being able to ask you this question.

John: We do not disappear in dreamless sleep. The mind is quiet. That is all. Your being and awareness remain. Otherwise, how do you wake up in the morning? This is more of a theoretical issue which sometimes comes up. The doubt is not of much practical consequence. You are undoubtedly alive and aware right now, and it is a matter of getting clear about what you are. That can be addressed here and now in the waking state.

The whole intent of the pointer is to highlight the fact that something in you remains constant throughout the passing of thoughts, feelings and perceptions. Whatever that is, is present here in the waking state, so you only need to be concerned with present experience. The whole issue boils down to the Question: What in you is present and aware of thoughts, perceptions, emotions and experiences? That is what you truly are. To get clear on that matter of your identity unravels the doubts and suffering that we experience.

Q: Thank you for responding to my question. I have read some of the writings on your web site. I, like you, have been studying this stuff for many years. When I did my own analysis of what I knew to be true, it appeared apparent that we are consciousness and that our awareness of our consciousness might be the highest state of normal consciousness.

John: I would suggest dropping the labels of 'consciousness' versus 'awareness' and 'higher' versus 'normal' states and so on. It is only just awareness. That aware-presence that you are, and which is knowing the mind, is what is being pointed to.

Q: I still tend to get sucked into my thinking and it feels as if I spend most of my time there. The way that I experience my life is probably way less painful then the average person, who thinks that everything that they think about is real, but I seem to be stuck in this place where I get it but keep getting caught in my thinking.

John: This is the rub. The roots of suffering need to be thoroughly unearthed. Otherwise, however clear the insights may be, we come back around to the residual doubts and suffering.

Q: That is where the question about dreaming comes up. To have an understanding and even the experience of awareness as reality does not seem real when it keeps slipping away. Why does it keep slipping away, and why are we not aware when we sleep if we are awareness? The fact that we are not aware when we sleep seems to point to the fact that awareness must be a function of the body and not an independent something that is us.

John: This is actually a diversion away from the inquiry into the origin and resolution of suffering. It is an interesting inquiry, but it can end up being more of speculation without a lot of practical impact on daily life.

As a side note, since you brought it up, awareness does not keep slipping away. Nor is it true to say that we are not aware in deep sleep. You most certainly are aware and present in sleep. Otherwise, how can you know a thought or dream when it appears in that state? It is just that the mind or senses have subsided temporarily. No one denies their own continued existence through sleep. The problem is that we focus on the thoughts or experiences. When they subside we falsely believe that awareness subsides. That is because we are conditioned to look at the objects and overlook the subject. Still, this is something of an academic pursuit, and, as you have found, does not necessarily lead to real freedom or insight.

You exist in the waking state, so I would suggest that for the time being you pursue the realization of your true nature in the waking state. Your existence and awareness now are beyond doubt. Besides, you need to inquire into the roots of suffering now, not in the deep sleep state, where the questions and doubts do not arise!

Q: I know that your basic teaching is to be present to the part of us that is aware of our thoughts and experiences. I can sit here at my computer and sense that part of myself and yet, nothing changes. My experience of life does not change.

John: That is because you are taking this fairly superficially. Be willing to probe into that seeming nothingness that you are and see what it has to reveal. It appears to be insignificant, at least to the mind that is accustomed to grosser states and experiences, but if you stay with it you will find immense depth and richness there.

61

False Concepts Must Be Questioned

Question: John, you wrote:

> *'Your nature as that natural clarity of presence-awareness does not conform to any of the concepts the mind asserts is what you are. No mind-created labels apply to awareness. Awareness is not an object. It has no phenomenal characteristics. You are awareness. How can the spacious, clear no-thingness of presence awareness have any mind-created labels and attributes? Is the clear sky of awareness, which is what you are, good or bad, enlightened or unenlightened, high or low?'*

I see that this essential point is what has been glossed over. The presence-awareness, seeing I am that and nothing else is not clear. I 'understand' I am that. But the clarity I glimpsed when we first met, and that I saw with Bob Adamson, is not stable and absolute, not in any real way. I sometimes despair that this will never be more than a concept. Asserting that 'I am that' seems to lead to moments of clarity, but I flop right back into conceptual knowing pretty quickly.

I listened to one of Bob Adamson's CDs yesterday and last night. Again, I get clarity, but it goes away and concepts are really all I have. So then in looking at who is thinking and so on, I get present to no thing. But it is a concept and not a living, thriving reality, as I have heard you describe it. I understand awareness has no objective attributes. But I do not see that. I much appreciate your help.

John: Can you deny the presence of awareness right now and in any moment? It is not a matter of seeing it or not. You do not see it or get it because you are it. It is more a brute undeniable fact. Everything that appears is just a movement in, on and through that presence-awareness. Recognize that without being-awareness, nothing can be. It is the base-line, the ultimate backstop. That is actually going on and is clearly present and evident upon a bit of looking in any moment. It cannot be grasped, understood, attained or achieved because all of those things are just conceptual movements that are floating in the very presence they are trying to grasp. All the seeking, getting, understanding and attaining are purely illusory concepts based on the idea that what you are seeking is not present. Those ideas are never fulfilled, because they are based on a misunderstanding. Waiting for 'enlightenment' is a fool's game because it will never 'happen'.

At this point, you do not need to see, get, know, understand, realize or find who you are. Awareness-presence is here. It is clear. And can you say that you are something apart from that? Is awareness one thing and you another? Everything that appears is just a display on that awareness, is just a movement or eruption arising within that. Nothing can be apart from that awareness. Show me anything with any substantial nature standing apart from its appearance in awareness.

Looking for awareness or trying to see it is like painting a rose, utterly redundant. It will tie the mind up in knots. That which is looking is the awareness itself. How can you look at or know anything without your own presence and awareness? Despite what the mind may believe, that awareness (you) is inherently unbound, unburdened, clear and free of problems. All problems, questions and doubts are basically thoughts. But awareness is innately free of thoughts and is ever untouched in its essence, just as the sky is not soiled by smoke, clouds, fog, leaves or anything passing through it.

All that you are dealing with now is false concepts that must be questioned and dismantled. See that when the focus goes onto the stories, labels and identifications in thoughts, the natural simplicity of awareness is traded for false thoughts. The belief and reality is placed into thought, and the mind scares itself out of its wits by taking its own imaginings as gospel truth. That is all that is happening. As far as I am concerned, this needs to be seen. Otherwise, we continue to fall for every sucker punch the mind throws at us. That is all we are dealing with at this point—getting fundamentally clear on our relationship with the mind and its thoughts, especially the self-centered thoughts.

Waiting for seeing or enlightenment is a delaying tactic because it postpones the dis-identification with (or questioning of) thought. The mind gets wrapped up in all the spiritual jargon and glorious anticipated experiences, yet the mechanism of suffering sails in under the radar and stays completely unexamined. This was my experience, which Bob Adamson finally exposed very clearly and beautifully to me.

See all suffering, doubts, questions, problems, issues, imagined attainments and losses as movements in the mind. They are all thought generated. Apart from thoughts, those things have no existence whatsoever. Nail this insight completely. Do not move from this until it is absolutely clear. There is nothing wrong with the body, mind, world or other people at any time. Fighting with those things is completely futile. All problems are the mind's labels, judgments and interpretations. We must see that all problems are sustained and created by the mind which is fabricating them. That is one aspect. Believing the thoughts to be true is where the real bondage arises, because if you do not believe them, they have no power. But first you need to clearly see what you are dealing with—thoughts, pure and simple.

At this point, I am more interested in you completely nailing the roots, origin and resolution of suffering rather then focusing on some imagined state of enlightenment or getting something. Once you understand the mechanism of suffering as clearly as the back of your hand, you will come to see that the pursuit of awakening or enlightenment is just another self-centered thought which generates its own suffering and doubt. But if you do not see the basics of suffering, you will not be able to see this. And the ongoing suffering will propel you to seeking imagined antidotes like enlightenment. However, as we start to see, those things never happen and never have worked.

62

Everything Settles in Naturally

Question: Well, it happened. I really took to heart the ideas you presented—that awareness is, that it cannot be obscured by thoughts and that all that keeps me from knowing myself is the idea that a separate person exists.

I inquired deeply, looking for this separate person, and what I found each time was awareness watching. For example, 'Who is this separate person who feels sad?' I would find no one. And in its place, I found awareness, unaffected by the sadness. I followed this line for a while and suddenly realized, 'Oh my God, Ramana calls it 'the Self'!—that is, this experience of joyful awareness that I seem to 'have' when I meditate is actually me!

It was profound—and simple. And this recognition seems to be lingering. My mind assumed that once realization occurred, there would be a continuous state, as if I would walk around in bliss. What I am finding is that I am pretty much the same, except that there is this baseline of peace. I still have many of my quirks and desires (or, more accurately, they exist within the field). Most of my major hang ups have vanished or are 90% weaker.

The irony is that now that I see myself as just empty-full peaceful awareness, I am finding it much easier to pursue 'my' goals now! On the one hand, I care even less about them, and on the other hand, there is all this extra energy, excitement and relaxation for them! In some funny way, I feel normal, like everything is finally OK. Now I can just go on living life, with a lot less fuss. When I look, the self does not seem to give a shit whether I kill people, feed the hungry, do nothing or pursue these goals.

John: Everything settles in naturally. You see, I told you how simple and easy this is! People often do not believe me, but then they stop and have a look at the basic pointers and find that it all does make sense. The best proof is your own direct sense of happiness and freedom that comes as a result of getting clear on the fundamentals of what you are and what you are not.

Q: My question now is, is there any relation between the natural state and action?

John: Actions just come up spontaneously in the awareness that you are. That is about it. The body and mind find their own balance and expression pretty effortlessly when the focus is off of the dualistic and self-centered thinking, just as your heart is effortlessly beating right now! Pretty easy!

Q: Is there any relation between my self and these goals, my actions, my words, my thoughts—other then them being objects in me, in 'my' awareness?

John: You are right to quote the word 'my'. The whole essence is that there is no such thing as a 'me' even present. It is not 'my awareness' or 'my body', but just awareness and a body. The separate self is liquidated from the picture, because it simply is not there. When that is seen as not present, all the self-centered thoughts, doubts and problems evaporate along with the imagined self.

63

Hold Onto the Fact of Your Own Being

Question: When the trading awareness for false thoughts is happening, I do not see it at the time. It is like a blindness. The understanding always arrives 'later'. During the period of 'trading', I am gonzo. All the understanding and clear seeing has completely been lost in the identity as a mind-bound entity.

John: It is important to nail down the fact that all suffering is just an arising in the mind, as a self-centered thought. The focus goes on that due to habit and gives the appearance that peace and clarity are not present. But is this true? The habit has us by the throat until questioned. This is not about 'getting it' or some future understanding. It is about a brute fact. Does awareness-being come and go or not? Period. Does awareness get clouded over by thoughts? Yes or no? This is not an attainment or a moment of insight when something 'shifts'. It is more basic and more profound than this.

Once you have pierced through the belief in the reality of thought and seen it for what it is, you cannot turn back. At that point, all you are dealing with is residual habits of mind. But now you know they are habits. They cannot dominate you like they did. Then come back and look, truly look, at your being. Thoughts arise and set in presence-awareness. No matter how many thoughts arise, they do not obscure the fact being pointed to. Use whatever analogy works—the mirror and the reflections, the sun and the clouds, the sky and the clouds. This is pointed out as a brute fact—you are already free, as that untouched presence-awareness. Thoughts of getting it and losing it are irrelevant. Even the thought 'I only see it after the event' is a concept rising in present awareness. Do you see that? The mind will tempt you to fall for that thought, as if it 'means' something, proves that you are not there and so on. Can you see the trick? That itself is a thought appearing in present, clear awareness. You will come to see all these tricks and ruses of thought. They are all calculated to show how you are not there yet, something needs to happen or you are missing something. These are all concepts arising in totally clear, doubtless awareness—now.

You may have spent years believing and pampering the mind. Now you must refuse to grant reality to beliefs in the mind. This is not assertion. It is faith and confidence based on your direct experience and knowing. It is having courage to take a stand on the deeper presence of truth within you based on your intuition, trust in the great teachings that have resonated so strongly, and a willingness to gamble that these pointers are true, not as a matter of blind belief, but in order to verify them for yourself. Make a firm and bold decision to take your stand as that reality transcending the mind. Disbelieve the habitual limited thoughts. Question and discard all self-centered thoughts and ideas.

Q: What puzzles me is, how can this be remembered at the times of obscuration of the awareness?

John: Do not worry about this. It is a false pursuit. See this in your moments of lucidity and everything will take care of itself. If the apparent seeing is obscured, it is obscured, and there is nothing you can do about it. So why worry? But the moment that you realize it is (seemingly) obscured, look into this and inquire what is obscured? What is this about? Awareness. Is that obscured right now? That is all that matters. Everything else is a concept, a delaying tactic. Review the fundamentals until the basics are part of the fabric of your outlook on life. Completely nail the origin, cause and resolution of suffering.

Q: But the dream seems real!

John: At least you are saying 'seems'. Yes, it seems real, because we believe it. Just as a snake imagined in the rope seems real. Just as the bogey man seems real. The key is that just because something seems real, does not mean it is real. You need to be willing and interested enough to question. Otherwise, you will never pierce through these concepts and feelings. Talking to spiritual friends is helpful at this point because you will keep getting feedback from outside the conceptual loop that the beliefs are not real. It is not the words. It is the confidence, the energy, the experience coming through that is key. It is the confirmation that a state exists outside the conceptual framework.

Q: After the storm subsides this is clear.

John: Good. Now dig into this one. Does the presence of clouds block the sun? Do your thoughts and emotional states obscure the fact of being? If you focus on the clouds and give all the reality to the clouds, you will be lamenting clouds forever. Turn to the sun and the clouds become irrelevant. Do not get into a fight with thoughts. Shift the focus to that which is already free of thoughts. It is like a jet piercing through the clouds and suddenly it is all clear and open. You do not get free, you discover, through deep looking, your already-present freedom. Then thoughts are not relevant. Thoughts being present or not makes no difference.

Q: But during the mind-bound thought-storms it is not clear!

John: Careful now. Did the fact of presence-awareness leave? See this now. Deeply see this.

Q: This flip-flopping is what makes me nuts!

John: Do not fall for this. Me? Nuts? Sounds like a pile of self-centered thoughts floating in this that is ever-free and clear. See it now. Flip-flopping is a total illusion. It is because all the focus is going into the mind. Put it at the real source, the awareness itself and the getting it and losing it are finished. This is can be realized in one moment of clear seeing of what is going on. So look until it is seen, and you will be done with this forever.

Q: I guess I need to keep looking until, as you say, it is nailed down for good, so long as there is any doubt remaining. And there still is sometimes when this is lost in a train of thought that links onto other trains. Then it obviously leaves the cake half baked.

John: Yes, the focus goes onto self-centered thoughts and the ever-present clarity that can never leave—ever—is overlooked. Priceless diamonds are traded for worthless clods of dirt. Once this is seen, you will be unable to make that trade, even if you want to. The game is up. Question everything that the mind says about who you are. Hold onto the one thing that cannot be questioned, the undeniable fact of your own being.

64

Doership, Responsibility and Judgment

Question: You say this approach is not advocating a neglect of doing the needful and common sense things demanded of the moment. I automatically feel tension when I read that because it feels like I am the doer who needs to do certain things to resolve the situation.

John: Not really. You are not the doer. The body and mind do what need to be done. There is no need to get in there as the doer or even the non-doer. Both are concepts. The body and mind are quite capable of taking appropriate action. That is what they are for!

Q: If say for instance, I sit on the couch all day ...

John: The body will get up and work and do something eventually. If you say 'I sit on the couch', then you are taking the body as your real nature. But are you the body or something more?

Q: But if I do nothing to resolve situations, then I would feel so lazy and bad!

John: With the sense of doer-ship and responsibility, the mind then creates judgments about whether it has met the mark and so on. Then the bad feelings arise. This is all just conceptual thought based on being a limited separate self, followed by judging the actions of that fictional character!

Q: But surely if there is no separate me it does not matter whether I sit there or not!

John: If there is no separate 'me', then who is sitting there? Who has an opinion of what matters? Get the false notion of being a separate 'me' out of the way and the body and mind will carry on quite well without any idea of a 'poor, limited me' in the picture. Believe me, all the necessary actions will go on quite well, even without the belief in the 'me'.

Q: Then ultimately it does not matter whether my husband finds work or we lose the house?

John: Sure it matters—to the family, to the landlord, to the tax collector! Your husband (or maybe even you!) will go out and do what needs to be done, not because of an 'I' but because the situation demands it. You are mixing up levels, mixing up apples and oranges. Action goes on quite well without false self-concepts.

Q: Is everything as it should be at all times?

John: You could say so. I would remove the judgment and say everything is as it is, including finding work or whatever needs to happen. Do the needful as demanded in the moment. Just do not forget your real nature.

Follow up ...

Q: Thanks for your reply. No more questions. It is now so clear.

65

Doubts, Time and the Separate Self

Question: There are still doubts. The tendency has been to ignore them as just old concepts arising, concepts that I can never resolve.

John: If the belief in the self-center is still active, the doubts will continue to arise. They are caused and sustained by that core belief. If you can ignore them that is fine, but if the root driver (the core 'I' concept) is not seen as false, the ignoring will not completely work.

Q: It seems that this tendency may be the mind playing tricks, because it seems like a cop-out. It is too easy to ignore the doubts when there are no consequences to putting off investigating them, for example, when everything is going smoothly in life.

John: The basic thing is that the potential for the doubts and questions to arise is in play, so the certitude is lacking. Even when everything is going right, there can still be anxiety for myself and my happiness, if not now then in the future.

Q: It occurred to me that the core doubt has to do with what you stated once, 'You are and you know that you are'. Yes, that is undeniable and the most solid factor in experience, but the doubt has to do with the future, the uncertainty about whether this existence will come to an end.

John: See that the future is just a concept arising in present awareness. Time, including both past and future, is always imagined in the present. Once that notion of the future is created in thought, then the mind worries that our existence may come to an end in that imagined future. But it is really all just mind stuff. When have you actually experienced any such thing as a 'future' except as a concept?

Q: Perhaps that is the basis of all other uncertainties.

John: Close but no cigar! The basis of all the uncertainties is the sense of 'I', the sense of being a separate self. The anxiety for the future is not about the future per se, but about the 'I' that we believe will experience the future and the imagined problems in it. Of what concern is the future without anyone to which it applies?

Q: The attachment to a continued and perpetual personal existence has not been given up, even though intellectually I see that everything is impermanent.

John: Yes, but as you are seeing, there can still be the residual belief in a separately existing self and our identity as that. It floats at the edge of peripheral vision, so to speak. It is a tacit assumption that somehow I am present as a tangible, separate something. The anxiety about the future is an indicator that that concept is in play and needs to be investigated. If there is no separate self, who would be anxious and about what? So probe a little deeper into this notion. If there is a self, that is, if you are a limited separate something or other, what is it and where is it?

Q: I have seen this attachment to self especially clearly when I have been depressed, and wishing for that 'joy of life' to return. There is a wishing for a carefree state with an open future. When it returned, I realized how attached I was to it.

John: Yes, this is still looking for happiness in an imagined future, which I am pointing out as being completely non-existent. You need to look more closely at the mechanism of suffering. Exclusive focus on self-centered thinking seems to obscure the ever-present state of freedom that is your true nature. To trace the roots of suffering to the imaginary self-center and investigate the reality of that concept brings the curtain down on the whole production.

Contradictory Pointers

Question: I am still puzzled by one question. If there is only presence-awareness, and if it is omnipresence and omnipotence, why do you invite seekers to 'have the willingness' to investigate and to see through something? Another teacher speaks about 'seeing through' as not the same as 'see through'. In one case, there is still someone. In the other, nobody. There is a huge difference in the two as pointers. You seem to talk to somebody, an individual. But at the same time, you say there is no doer. Why this contradiction? You already answered me on this point a few months ago, but it is not yet clear for me. Other teachers are clearer. They do not speak to anybody. There is no recommendation whatsoever. They speak about a description rather a prescription for awareness. This is a crucial point for me to get clarity.

John: All words and pointers are contradictory because they are just symbols pointing to something. Even the clearest words are full of holes and contradictions, if you look deeply at them. But this is the nature of words and pointers. Forget words. Know yourself as undeniable presence-awareness. That is all there is, and you are that. Any doubts about that?

Q: Thank you, but for you are 'seeing through' and 'you must have the willingness to see through', the same pointers? I see a huge difference, although both are just concepts.

John: They are all just concepts. To analyze concepts for their characteristics and differences will keep you spinning in thought. What in you is aware of thoughts and concepts?

That is what the words are pointing to. The answer is not in the mind. It is the non-conceptual recognition of present awareness, which is what you are.

67

'Self' Versus 'I'?

Question: I thought that I would never have another question, but guess what? One came up. Here it is. Following a discussion with a friend, I wrote 'Each of us does have a separate self, that is, an operationally separate body and mind that of course is not separate from, and is completely one with air, food, perceptions, and experiences derived from a supposedly outside world. When a male body and a female body get into bed together, it is a quite different experience than when one body moves into bed by itself. Your emotionality is distinct from mine, which is distinct from everyone else's'. In other words, I asserted that parts make up the whole and that all parts are functioning as one within the whole. Therefore, both a 'separate self' and 'no self' are true.

I wrote another long paragraph positing that the 'self' is not the 'I', and that a failure to make this distinction is perhaps the gravest confusion of all seekers. Because the 'self' appears to arise moment-by-moment, and does not last forever, that does not imply that it is not existentially 'real'. Each person can appreciate and honor his or her 'own' uniqueness. My friend told me that the distinction between a 'self' and the 'I-thought' was phony. But I replied that everyone required a sound pointing to the distinction between the 'self' and the 'I'.

In other words, are 'appearances' real, including emotional tendencies, predilections, perceptions and experiences? I say that all comes from source, pure awareness, the base and container, and that no identifiable 'I' exists except as a passing thought. Yet 'selves' do exist. In contrast, you [John] write, 'Look for the separate self and you find it entirely absent'. By 'separate self' do you mean those patterns of thought, and styles of walking, dressing, communicating, and behaving that clearly demonstrate a unique entity different from another? Or by your quote do you mean a false sense of 'I' that seizes thoughts and emotions and produces a thought-chain of suffering? Am I wrong when I say that this body-mind is a male and not a female? Is it proper for me to walk into a ladies restroom? As another example of 'my' self, in this lifetime I will never make it as a mathematician.

Today, after my friend and I spoke, I sensed that he did have something valuable to say about 'no self'. The rest of the day I felt one with the environment in a fuller sense than I have ever experienced. Some blockage had released. Maybe there is some unreal 'self' sense that is not totally washed away. Yet trashing the part because it vanishes into the whole obfuscates the personal realities that require examination and even change. In fact, I love to change outmoded attitudes and behaviors.

In this context of 'self' and 'no-self', do you distinguish between a 'self' and an 'I'? The last thing I want is to become involved with meaningless argumentation about abstruse metaphysical concepts. Somehow, my friend's statements resonated both as 'no' and 'yes' with me. I would appreciate your thoughts about this real (or false) distinction between an 'I' and a 'self'.

John: All questions and doubts are just thoughts. They are just ripples arising in the ever-clear and present awareness that you are. They have no real existence. Their substance is nothing but that awareness itself. That awareness is, and it is beyond any and all doubts whatsoever. That is what you are. That is the ultimate view that annihilates any doubts. To look in this way does not address the subject or topic of the doubts, but shifts the focus to the doubtless awareness in which all thoughts arise, and it points out your nature as that. From this position, doubts are more or less annihilated outright, like moths plunging into a flame. There is nothing left to talk about!

When we begin to debate the meaning of thoughts we are clearly stepping into the mind level, and we are then dealing with provisional topics subject to effects of language, interpretation and semantics. Ultimately, it is all just concepts and words. They are all only symbols that are dead and inert in themselves. The words 'I' and 'self'—what are these really except symbolic images rippling in awareness or noises moving through the air? What they are pointing to is anybody's guess. It is all based on the interpretation given to those ideas.

When I say there is no self or no 'I', it simply means that there is no particular thing, object, thought, experience, emotion, state and so on that we can grasp hold of and say this is me, this is what I am. Of course there are bodies, thoughts, experiences arising and setting in awareness. But am I prepared to say that any of those things are the essence of what I am, in and of themselves? How can they be when I am that awareness in which those things arise? This is all I mean when I say that there is no self.

If I label the particular confluence of sensations and experiences of this body, this locus of perception and action, as John Wheeler and call it me, that is strictly a convenience of communication. There is clearly nothing abiding or enduring in those things, and they certainly are not the essence of myself, my true being, which is that presence of awareness or being that remains regardless of the flow of transient experiences. In this respect, the body is not a 'self' in the sense that I am using the word. This analysis holds for the thoughts, emotions and sensations as well. And I have yet to find anything that is not a thought, emotion, sensation or combination of these.

If you say that the body-mind has traits, characteristics, habits, and so on that is reasonable. Why not? Just do not call those things who and what you are. If you do, there is a basic mis-identification of your real being with those things, which are clearly not your essence. Looking in this way, the body and mind do not constitute anything approaching a self. Of course, one can use the term 'self' in anyway that suits one, and I think the issue is, in fact, largely one of semantics.

So the body, senses, mind and so forth do not constitute 'I'. Yet we constantly speak of 'I' this and 'I' that. What are we talking about? Where is this thing, this 'I' entity? We say 'I' am John, 'I' am a male, 'I' am this, 'I' am that. What is this chameleon-like I-thought which willy-nilly gets appended to such disparate traits and characteristics? What is the thing in itself? Basically 'I' is a word, a concept, a label with no referent, no particular thing that it points to. So there is the word 'I', but there is no particularly thing that is the 'I'. There is no particular thing in the appearance that is what you are. It is all non-self, non 'I'. You, as an entity or separate self in the appearance, do not exist. What you are in terms of the appearance is a complete absence, an emptiness.

To say that the appearance of bodies in awareness constitute so many separate selves is either 1) just a convention of language for the purpose of communication, which is fine, if understood as such, or 2) may belie a superficial understanding of the issue. The great spiritual traditions have clearly articulated that the notion of separate selfhood is the root of ignorance and suffering. They clearly and with one voice have consistently and completely refuted the existence of an individual self, ego or person and stated that this very notion is the core of the metaphysical problem.

But of course you most tangibly are, as that indisputable presence-awareness. It is present and inescapable. It is that 'cognizing emptiness' that is the space in which all forms are appearing. All forms, bodies and experiences are arising at the same level of appearance. How can we even make the distinction as to which is you and not you when they are all arising as ripples in the one space of awareness that you are? You could make a reasonable case that all of the appearances are who you are, or that none of them are who are you are. But to slice off one bit of the appearance, one body-mind, and call it 'me' is unwarranted.

However, keep in mind that all this verbiage is just a bunch of movement in thought! Everything is reducible to thoughts arising and setting in awareness. Thoughts themselves are like waves arising and setting in the awareness that you are. They are made of that. So all there is, really, is only that one awareness and nothing else. So what is to debate and with whom? All there is, is the undeniable, inescapable fact of presence-awareness. Nothing exists apart from that. You are that. That is pure serenity and clarity at all times. Doubts never touch that, just as clouds never touch the sun.

68

Wavering and Recognition

Question: A question that arises is about wavering. It is my experience (from inquiring) that awareness is always there. And, it is my experience that I am that! That feels good to say.

John: Excellent.

Q: Some days there is a clearer recognition of my true nature.

John: Awareness, your actual being, remains steady and rock-solid at all times. It needs no recognition at all. It is simply the undoubtable and ever-present canvas that the painting of the world displays upon. There is no separate someone who needs to recognize it. It is what you are.

Q: Some days there is more recognition of awareness than others.

John: If the mind wanders into self-centered thoughts, a bit of focus goes into them, but it does not change the ever-present fact of being-awareness. There is no recognition of awareness. That is a dualistic concept, really. Even when there is seemingly no recognition of awareness, how do you know that? It appears as an arising in awareness! Just see this clearly. Verify it until the basic point is clear. Then there is no wavering.

Q: My mind hoped that once I saw my Self it would never waver!

John: Mind? I? Self? There are too many variables here! You do not see the Self (that is, yourself), you are the Self. Period and full stop! Your being as that undeniable presence of awareness never wavers.

Q: I had hoped that the mind would not generate more problems or re-formulate an identity. Unfortunately it has!

John: There may be some residual self-centered beliefs arising due to habit and a bit of belief going into them. That is all. So question a bit and come back to the fact that you are not a limited self at all. There is no entity there with a problem. The self-centered thoughts are sustained through a belief in the reality of a separate self at the core. Did you find one—ever? And can you doubt the fact of your being-awareness? Seeing this, there is no problem. Thoughts arise in the ever-clear presence-awareness that you are. Let them arise! Do the clouds ever touch the sun?

Q: I admit that the problems are not there as much, as deeply or for as long now.

John: Good. The doubts and problems naturally drop out of the picture once the true position is seen. Stay with the basics. Confirm them until everything is clear and beyond doubt.

69

Pain, Suffering and Perfection

Question: Thank you so much for the book *Awakening to the Natural State*, which I am very much enjoying. There has been a gradual growing awareness of and as presence. This is it. And for some time there has been a sense that perfection is, no matter what arises.

John: For a time we are focused on the appearances that are arising. Time arises in the appearance, along with various objects and experiences that the mind labels as perfect (or not!). But what is being pointed to is your true essence, the fact of being-awareness, the light of presence-awareness which is illumining the display of appearances. That is, and ever remains, regardless of the appearances. That is you, your true nature. You are that perfection. Perfection, presence, awareness, and so on are just words pointing to the fact of your inherently perfect real nature. Everything that can arise appears as a display or projection in and on the bright, luminous clear presence that you are. This is present and utterly beyond doubt at all times. You are that, and you are fully, totally free right now.

Q: Paradoxically, the false sense of 'I' and associated thoughts also sometimes arise saying, 'But it would be better if…' and so on.

John: These are only thoughts arising in the perfect clarity of presence-awareness that you are.

Q: Increasingly, awareness is that which observes this coming and going.

John: Drop the word 'increasingly'. This is unnecessary. All thoughts, for everyone and at all times, are known in awareness. How else are they known? It is just a fact that is seen with a bit of investigation. This is not about movements towards an anticipated state of clarity or freedom in the future. It is recognizing what is true and clear in you now.

Q: There has been an apparently growing recognition that 'this is it' by the seeing that perfection, which is beyond perfection and no perfection, simply is no matter what comes up (for example, pain, distress, lack of cash and so on)

John: Just be clear that 'it' or 'perfection' (or whatever the term used) is the fact of your being. You are and you remain as the principle of presence-awareness on which all experiences appear and disappear. You are totally untouched, just as the sky is untouched by passing clouds. It is simply a fact that is pointed out. Awareness does not come and go with the arising and passing of content in awareness. It just does not!

Q: So when I read in your book 'the approach of saying that all suffering and separation is part of the oneness, so just let them be there, is not particularly liberating' I was somewhat confused and disappointed. This does not seem to be what is experienced here.

John: The confusion and disappointment comes up because the ideas presented do not match the formulation that the mind expects! But this is still looking in the mind for some kind of confirmation or answer. Throughout all of this, did you cease to exist, cease to be present and aware? Could my words or descriptions knock you out of the fact of your own being? All of the words, doubts and feelings are dancing right in you, your doubtless existence, which is present and brightly aware. That is all that is being pointed to.

Q: I do feel that what you are saying is OK.

John: I am pointing to that in you which is beyond the mind and not subject to doubts and cannot be eclipsed by passing experiences. My words may be inadequate, but the fact of your being is beyond all doubt.

Q: Do you mean the following? Suffering arises …

John: By suffering, I mean doubts, questions, problems, fears, anxieties and so on arising from the mistaken belief that you are a limited separate entity standing apart from pure being-awareness. This suffering arises in the mind as thoughts based on that fundamental erroneous concept. They are generated by a conceptual error. When that error is corrected through clear seeing, the subsequent thoughts based on that error are removed. They are neither right nor wrong, perfect or imperfect. They are simply effects based on a misperception.

Q: Well, take the case of a pain apparently in the body.

John: This is just a physical fact. There is no suffering, as I have defined it above, in this. It may not be pleasant, but keep in mind there is a difference between physical pain and suffering.

Q: I can see by direct experience that the pain is in the space. The body is also in the space.

John: I am not sure what you are getting at here. The pain is just a movement of energy, a vibration, an event appearing in the space of awareness. Awareness is not touched. It is just like a cloud does not really effect the sky.

Q: There is a noticing of the pain.

John: This is just a natural function.

Q: Then there may be a thought that says 'uncomfortable' and another thought that says 'see the doctor, take a pill' or whatever.

John: These are all reasonable thoughts that may arise in response to the event. There is still no particular suffering involved at this stage.

Q: The pain is, as one teacher would say, the invitation to see that there is no one to suffer.

John: Pain is pain. Suffering arises from the belief that I am limited, separate entity to whom the pain arises. The pain is irrelevant. A pleasant sensation can trigger the same self-centered train of illusory concepts stemming from the belief in an existent 'me'. There is no 'me' at all. There is only the experience, but no one who is experiencing. Seeing this, the root cause of the suffering, the assumed self-center, is exposed. In truth, it is completely liquidated along with the psychological suffering generated by that belief.

Q: The self-expanding space sweeps away the sense that there is a 'me'. As this is recognized, the pain falls away (maybe apparently via the pill taken) because the pain is no longer necessary. It is no longer the only way that perfection or oneness can be recognized. It is seen that one never left home.

John: Who says the physical pain would disappear? It may or may not. That is not an issue. If it stays, it stays. If it goes, it goes. Who is choosing? However, with the belief in the 'me' removed through clear seeing, the self-centered thoughts and attendant suffering based on that false belief surely fall away. On that score, I would agree with you.

Q: One is home and there is no person.

John: Yes. That is what is being pointed to as the present condition. We just believe otherwise and suffer needlessly for some period of time until we investigate and see the truth of things. Awareness is. Everything is that. You are that. All suffering, doubts, questions and problems are for someone, a person. Those thought-created concepts survive because we believe there is a person. However, there is no separate person. Seeing this, all the false notions dependent on that core belief are annihilated in that seeing.

Q: In a sense, the so-called suffering is in fact perfection because it is a pulling us back to that which is, perfection itself.

John: Sure, you can see suffering as a reminder that points you back to the perfection itself. Everything is a movement in and of that. At this point, we are dealing with different 'styles' of pointers. Find one that works and resonates. The way I talk about this is what worked for me. I am not claiming this is the only way to talk about this. You can say suffering is the perfection or you can say that suffering is the result of an erroneous concept. They are both just pointers. Either one brings you back to the fact of the recognition of the perfection itself, which is all there is, and you are that. Seeing this, the suffering born of the imagination of separation is resolved.

Thoughts Cannot Reflect the Truth

Question: From reading your articles, I see two main points you are trying to make First, that there is no 'me'. Second, that we are awareness only.

John: Fair enough! However, for the record, I would place emphasis on the fact of awareness. That is first and primary. All other experiences or understandings can only be by virtue of the presence of awareness. Me or no me, awareness ever is.

Q: In trying to have the thoughts reflect the truth …

John: This is unnecessary. In fact, it will hang you up. Thoughts cannot reflect the truth. Thoughts are words and symbols. You are that presence-awareness that is upstream of thoughts. It cannot be caught in words. To recognize the fact of your being is not through thought. It is immediate, non-conceptual knowledge.

Q: I was going to say that I can only really focus on one of these points at a time.

John: Correct. However, the intent is not for you to focus on thoughts but to recognize your own true nature, which is not a thought. So do not look in the wrong direction!

Q: In the past, glimpses that I have had came after reading that there is no 'me'.

John: Yes, there is nothing at all that is a separate self. The belief in a 'me' is the core mistaken concept.

Q: But the separation comes back.

John: The belief in the existent 'me' is what generates the separation feeling. You need to finally expose that concept.

Q: Are these supposed to be two separate paths to what is pointed to, or are they supposed to be one pointer?

John: It is like two sides of a coin. There is the truth of what you are: being-awareness. There is the false idea of what you imagine yourself to be: a limited, separate self. Both pointers support and reinforce each other.

Q: You seem to talk about only one of them at a time.

John: Yes, it is hard to talk about two things at the same time!

Q: The link between the two points is not so clear for me, either. Could you marry the two points for me?

John: Not recognizing our true nature, there is a false belief in what we are not (a separate, limited self). The belief and focus on the apparent false self keeps us from seeing the ever-present clarity of our true nature. The belief in the separate self is the root of suffering. To deconstruct that belief uproots the source of doubts and suffering. That goes hand-in-hand with the recognition of what is clear and present within us. Use both pointers or either one—or none! You do not need any pointers or paths to be what you are. It all gets back to the recognition of your real nature.

Your Identity Is Clear—Now

Question: I was on your site and noticed you using the phrase 'being-awareness'. I like that. It resonates. The mind wants to turn it around into 'awareness-being', which slides dangerously into noun-hood or thingness.

John: I use both (and more!): awareness-being, being-awareness, presence-awareness, awareness-presence. They are all good! They are just words, labels or pointers to your true nature.

Q: When it gets right down to it, the words of Ramana still bug me—that so few ever move past an intellectual understanding. And even when I drop the word 'intellectual', I know what I know, but I still feel, well, on the mind-knowing side of things.

John: The basic point is that you are that which is knowing the mind. The mind, which is just a name for the collection of passing thoughts, is your object. You are aware of it. The immediate knowledge of yourself, which is clearly present and brightly aware, is always on the side of non-conceptual, non-intellectual experience. This is just a fact, which becomes clear with a little looking.

Q: I can hear your words and see your face saying, 'See this as all mind-stuff and drop it'. I do and can. But… Then I think, 'but what?'

John: You got it! If you have got buts coming up, they are being generated by some doubts and questions, so you need to get them out for inspection and resolution. No harm in that. If you can drop the questions, great. If not, get them resolved one way or another.

Q: When were you certain that awareness being was/is truly what you are, what everything is?

John: Are you present and aware right now? Yes or no? When did you become aware of this? It is. It is pointed out. In the recognition of the pointer, it is realized as the ever-present fact. 'When' is a concept based on the notion of time. It projects the recognition of present awareness into an imagined future, which never arrives! You do not need to manufacture present awareness, but you can dismantle a false concept by seeing it as false. Do it now! Awareness and your identity as that is actually clear—now. The simplicity of it is what people miss!

72

There Is No Separation at Any Time

Question: I have read *Awakening to the Natural State* and it is amazing. I am awaiting the delivery of *Shining in Plain View*. I came across this non-dual stuff about six months ago. My previous history featured thirty years of seeking, which seems fairly standard in the non-dual community.

John: Yes. Many of us poked around for a few years before we found the answer was right here under our noses. And we are grateful for getting it pointed out!

Q: Basically, yes, I agree with everything and understanding is complete.

John: Glad to hear it. Keep in mind that agreement is more or less a mental assent, which is fine in itself. Understanding is complete because the fact of presence, being or awareness (whatever label is used) is fully present and clear. It is that doubtless sense of being that no one can deny. In this sense, understanding is full and complete for everyone at all times.

Q: But old habits die hard!

John: No habits or doubts ever contradict what is being pointed to. Habits, doubts and all else arise in the immediate and ever-clear presence that you are. Seeing this is all that is needed. Until the simplicity of this is noticed, come back to the basic pointers and see them for yourself. It is also helpful to expose and dismantle contrary beliefs. Fixation on those beliefs keeps us looking away from the simplicity of what is being pointed to.

Q: I have just been reading your web site again and found the thought arising, 'Oh yes, of course. There is no me. There is only awareness'.

John: Thought or no thought, awareness is. It is that space of pure knowing in which all thought and non-thought arises.

Q: It is so obvious every time I read it or encounter it.

John: Yes. That is the beauty of it. Just keep in mind that it is not obvious because you read about it. It is obvious in and of itself. The statements or pointers are self-evident and immediately recognized as true.

Q: Then there appears to be a sliding back. As I write I can almost hear your answer (and that of some other teachers I am aware of). You (or they) might say, 'What is aware of sliding back?' Then there is awareness of awareness again, as it were.

John: Excellent seeing. You will find in looking at this that you are present and aware. That simply remains and abides as the container of all experiences. That is not separate from you, and it is, in fact, your real being or true essence. It is not something to become aware of because it is not an object that can be grasped or seen as if it were out in front of you. It is the undoubtable suchness or is-ness, the constant presence-awareness shining at the center always. The apparent deviation from this is just that, only an appearance, because you cannot leave the fact of your being. 'Sliding back' and 'awareness of awareness' are conceptual appearances arising and passing in the light of present awareness. Once you see what is being pointed to here, and it is very simple, the wavering is completely finished. We were just focused in the wrong direction, so to speak.

Q: Nonetheless, there seems to be something different about you guys. That apparent procedure does not happen. 'Awareness of awareness' never seems to become dim.

John: Right now, all of those ideas are just thoughts appearing in—what? You guessed it—the fact of present awareness. Come back to the consideration that your actual awareness as it is right now is never absent, never dimmed or covered over. Everything that can appear for everyone at all times is appearing in the presence of awareness. Not seeing this, the attention drifts into conceptual thoughts and mind stuff based on a belief that a separation from the source has occurred. However, there is no separation at any time. Just have a look and verify this to your satisfaction.

Q: I do not want to make anything special about this. I can see the mind trying to make something special out of 'other people' and that I cannot possibly attain it myself. That word 'attain' is so mind-based!

John: Good. This is clear for you. Do not make this a case of special people who have something you do not have. To follow that concept is just attending to a belief and looking away from the simplicity of what is being pointed to.

Q: I do not know if this is a forum, by the way, or if you still do email correspondence, so apologies if this is not the way things are done on your site. I live in England by the way. Do you ever get over to these parts to do talks? I find your writing particularly clear, incidentally. I love the way you answer questions and do not just dismiss the questioner as being intellectual. This was particularly impressive in *Awakening to the The Natural State* when you were asked the question about why it is that awareness only seems to be seeing out of a particular individual's eyes and not those of other apparent individuals. Your analogy about the dream was very clarifying. Thank you. With warmest wishes from an autumnal England.

John: Thanks for the note. Feel free to keep in touch if anything else comes up to share.

73

Pain and Present Perfection

Question: What you say about the difference between suffering and pain I find difficult to appreciate. Pain by its nature is uncomfortable.

John: Sure. Physical pain is not comfortable. Pain is the body's intelligence saying that something is wrong.

Q: If present perfection is, why would the body that arises in and as awareness not function accurately and painlessly?

John: Bodies are just transient forms subject to birth, change, disease, injury, old age and death. It is just part of the scheme of things. Who says there is anything wrong with it? It is part of the rhythm of things. If bodies did not pass on, the earth would be overrun with bodies. That is as much a part of the order of things as anything else. And there is not a bit of suffering in any of that. The body will function smoothly and (relatively!) painlessly as long as it is in good health. But that condition is not sustainable forever.

Q: Is my question moving into mind formulas again and away from present awareness?

John: Awareness is something else altogether. It is that perfection in which the body, mind and world rise and set. Seeing that, the body is free to come and go as it will, but the deeper perfection remains present all the while. Most of the fear regarding the body stems from identifying our true nature with the body.

To Whom Do Sensations Appear?

Question: Although I have always resonated more with your articles and correspondence on the point of there being no separate self, the point has grown weaker for me as time goes on. Phrases like 'there is no me' and 'there is no separate self' have become empty, intellectual points. The rational mind can say there is no 'me', but there is still identification going on.

John: It is not enough to think about all this. It is like reading about love. There may be some initial inspiration with the first reading, but no actual love comes from the words about it. The pointers are to something to be known or understood, not simply to be thought about.

The fact of identification still going is the key point. One very clear point to get from this is that thinking about things at an intellectual level has very little relation to the dissolution of identification. It is a good start, but there is more to it. You need to understand what identification is, where it comes from, how it operates. Otherwise, you are a slave to it.

Q: To break the identification, I try to watch the thoughts …

John: Watching thoughts is not enough. What is your intent in doing that? Identification consists in the unexamined ideas about who and what we are. Simply watching thoughts does not bring those concepts to light.

Q: I notice that I am still identified with the sensations of the head, and vice versa, when watching the sensations.

John: Watching sensations will not resolve the issue of your identity. There is not a causal link there, as I far as I am concerned.

Q: With regards to looking for the separate self—I cannot find one. But I feel that if I were the separate self, I would not be able to find it, just as the eyes cannot find themselves. Perhaps I am not clear on what the separate self is anymore. How else might I finally expose that concept?

John: I would recommend, based on my experience, to start with the positive knowledge of what you are. I view the recognition of no-self as a follow on to the positive recognition of what you are. Without some sense of the reality that is being pointed to, we are left trying to find an answer in the mind, that is, we are reduced to thinking about all this. As you have seen, that approach runs dry pretty quickly.

Q: I also have a problem recognizing the fact of 'my' being. It does seem more natural to recognize the fact of being, without the 'my'.

John: Good. The undeniable fact of being and awareness is here right now. That never comes and goes, and—like it or not!—is what you are. It is not an abstract principle out there, but is 'in here', shining in and through your eyes. It is so present that we overlook it.

Q: Every sense of my existence seems to rely on something else.

John: This is not true. You are first. Only then can other things appear. Without you being present and aware, how can there be anything else? We are very accustomed to look objectively, but what you are is not an object at all. It is that which is aware of objects. It is not mysterious and difficult. It is so obvious that we overlook the simplicity of it. Are you present? Are you aware? These cannot be doubted. There is something being pointed to there. What is that?

Q: But it is only after seeing that something else exists that we infer that awareness is present.

John: This is the obvious and predictable error that arises from overlooking the subjective element. Nothing else can be there or be known at all without awareness. Are you aware or not? Yes or no? Is that an inference? Is the fact of your being a mere hypothesis? You have to be present and aware even to think that!

Q: There is no obvious pure 'I am' sense.

John: Sure there is. Do you exist right now? Yes or no! Every child can answer that! Existence, awareness, presence-awareness or being-awareness—whatever the formulation—are words pointing to something. It is what this is all about. Miss this and you miss everything.

From the point of view of the mind, existence or awareness seems to be a nothingness. This is because the mind deals in objects and being-awareness is non-objective. That is why thinking about this is a dead-end. The answer is not in the mind. It is about the non-conceptual recognition of the fact of your own being. It sounds mysterious in words because words are objective and cannot capture what is being pointed to. As I say, it is shining in plain view. Yet, out of habit, we can look in the wrong direction and miss the essence of it.

Q: Everything seems to be appearances, sensations from the heart or head.

John: Yes, but to whom, or to what, do sensations appear? That is most certainly present, because a sensation does not appear to itself. That needs to be probed into a bit.

75

Why? and How? Are False Questions

Question: The last couple of years I have developed a bit of a loathing towards too much intellectualization, even though I often fall back into the trap that gets nowhere, that is, the mind.

John: Well, now you know that running this through the mind leads to an impasse. So you do not have to make that mistake any longer.

Q: On the other hand, I do experience the lightness of not getting too involved with the thought stream, even though I do not absolutely find myself free of all doubt and suffering. The minute my mind says that such freedom is impossible, I just see it as a passing thought that will not last long, and, sure enough, it does not.

John: I found it helpful to eventually tackle head on the question of what is the nature of doubt and suffering and really understand them. Obviously, they are arisings in the mind and have no other real existence.

Q: Of all the philosophies and religions, the non-dual pointers seem to make the most sense and hold the most promise. I know, that sounds contradictory, but our normal everyday language is full of these dualistic terms. I know that the hope of a future promise is dualistic mind stuff.

John: I prefer not to get too overly non-dualistic about things. It is possible to understand who you are and be free of doubts.

It is exciting that this is possible, and it is worth pursuing, in spite of what the politically correct non-dualist would say.

Q: Perhaps a whole new approach to even everyday language will soon be necessary. I find it most useful just to read your short articles and just sit with them.

John: Simply following the pointers and resonating with things in direct experience is really what it gets down to.

Q: One of the points that I have just realized I was hung up on, is that everything arises in awareness.

John: That is just a simple pointer to something that is evident upon a bit of looking. You are aware and everything you know arises as an experience in awareness. There are not too many moving parts to figure out or deal with with that one!

Q: I presume you are talking of the awareness that is neither yours nor mine, but that which is universal, which is responsible for the appearing of all forms and for the arising of all thoughts in every creature at any time or place in existence.

John: Yes, but that is much more wordy and conceptual than I think is necessary! It is just plain and simple awareness, the basic sense of knowingness. In and of itself it has no label such as 'universal', nor does it suffer from the notion of being responsible for anything. That is personalizing it and laying a concept on it. All thoughts and creatures are just experiences arising in this present awareness. In direct experience awareness is singular. We have no knowledge or experience of multiple awarenesses.

Q: So it is not something which we can get, because it has got us. Right?

John: More accurately, we are it. It is not a thing, a principle out there. Awareness is a quality or aspect of what you are. You are aware. It's good to bring the chickens home to roost. We are dealing with you, nothing else.

Q: And now, the million dollar question. How and why does the unlimited presence-awareness fool or limit itself into thinking that it is a limited mind-body mechanism?

John: This is an excellent question that shows you have been doing your homework. Looking in this way gets to the root of things very quickly. The direct answer is that limitation is only apparent and is not real. This becomes evident on a bit of looking. Even now, present awareness is unbound, unlimited and free of appearances. The seeming identification has not occurred. It is assumed to have occurred, but upon investigation it is seen that is has not. Also, the seeming solidly existing body-mind with which awareness supposedly identifies, when looked into, is seen to be just an appearance composed of nothing but awareness itself. It is all one substance, one essence. So there really is nothing substantial existing apart from awareness with which it could identify. What happens in looking this way is that the assumed problem dissolves. It is an error of understanding.

You can try to push back the scope of the question and ask, then why did the error of understanding arise? This is the same problem in a different form. You can see that the mind, at its own level, can keep generating all kinds of conceptual doubts. Yet when they are closely examined, you always find that the presuppositions upon which the questions are based are flawed and do not stand up to investigation. Basically, these kinds of questions are not answerable at the level at which they are asked. As I say, it is like asking when the man in the moon was born, when he got married and so on. The questions sound reasonable, but are really invalid because an erroneous belief is at work even in generating the question. For example, in this case, there is no man in the moon!

So, instead of asking how and why did awareness become limited (and assuming that it did), it is more effective to investigate if awareness is, in fact, limited or bound at all. If it is not, then the question just drops away, because it is invalid. You do not answer a false question. You discard it.

Another approach is simply to recognize that the question is arising in awareness. It is a thought, which is just a movement or appearance in awareness. It has no real existence apart from awareness. It arises in awareness and sets in awareness. Its substance or content is awareness itself. So what you are always dealing with is pure awareness at all times. Everything that appears is just that. So where is the separation? What can identify with what when it is all one substance? That awareness, or your real nature, is completely clear and evident now. Looking in this way brings you directly to the recognition of freedom and clarity immediately. In other words, it is the recognition of the non-dual presence-awareness itself here and now.

At a more relative level, the questions of 'why?' and 'how?' imply concepts such as time, causality, purpose, intent, reason and so on. So you can see that a question like this is implicitly riding on a host of concepts that are assumed as real, even for the question to be able to arise. Looking into all of these shows that they are categories or concepts created by the mind itself. Without thought they simply do not exist as independent realities in and of themselves. In short, they are not real. So the mind creates these concepts, and then, based on these concepts, generates questions and doubts. The conclusion is that the questions are not answerable because they are based on false assumptions or premises. This can be seen and understood, and in this seeing, the questions are exposed and fall away.

As a final pointer, you can see that the mind is trying to understand something which is completely outside of its domain. Thoughts arise in awareness. Awareness knows thoughts, but thought cannot know awareness. It is like a fly buzzing around on the inside of a window pane hoping to experience the vast sky beyond. The means are lacking. So at the end of the day, the whys, hows, buts, ifs and all the rest of the mind-generated questions are futile. The answer is not in the mind. The sooner this is recognized, the more directly you can relax the attempt to 'get it' with the mind.

Yet your being as awareness is clear, present, solid and utterly without doubt here and now. To recognize that as your true nature is what all the pointers are about. Let the focus come off the mind and relax with the natural recognition of the simple and obvious presence-awareness that you are.

73

Is This Another Dualistic Technique?

Question: Hi, John. It has been quite a while since I have written to you or read your site. Really, I have not been reading much of anything of a 'spiritual' nature lately. I was reading some of your email responses on your site. They are excellent as always. I really look forward to reading your new book.

One thing I have read recently is a prominent teacher's new book. In reading his book and your site (not that the two 'teachings', for lack of a better term, are the same!), the question I keep coming back to is this. This teacher talks about 'staying in the now', 'becoming aware of the inner body', 'watching the thinker', 'observing the pain-body', and so on. All of these things seem to be techniques.

John: This is all, as you may have guessed, very different from what I am presenting. Some comments:

'*Staying in the now*'. First of all, all there is, is the now. So you cannot really get out of it. Nor do you need to come back to it. In highest truth, the now is a concept. Present awareness is timeless. So the 'now' is either a) all there is, or b) not existent, depending on how you view it. There is no entity present as such who can get back to the now, ultimately.

'*Becoming aware of the inner body*'. There is no need to do this, as we are already aware of all the thoughts, feelings and sensations effortlessly. To try to become aware is trying to do something that is already happening.

'*Watch the thinker*'. There is no thinker, as such, only thoughts. To watch the thinker could be a hopeless task. I would say to first try to find such a thing. If the directive is to watch thoughts, again, that is already happening automatically.

'Observing the pain-body'. This is an interesting concept, apparently constructed by the author. At best it is way of trying to explain the origin of suffering by providing some kind of model or theory. All I would say is not to take the concept too seriously—as if there is such a thing as a pain-body. I have yet to see any such thing.

All of these pointers could be viewed as useful stepping stones to getting some basic understanding about ourselves, but there is some duality implied in them. They are not as simple and clear as I have found in other presentations. The proof is in the pudding, though. There is no harm in giving them a go and seeing what you come up with.

Q: I find (as does everyone else I know) that there are times it seems I am able to do these things and other times when I absolutely forget and get completely caught up in the mind-stream again.

John: That is the issue with techniques. You either forget them, or you cannot sustain them or they simply run out of juice. We have all been around that block many times, I would guess. Still they keep you looking and questioning and eventually an interest arises to get to the bottom of things.

Q: In a way, it seems that some of the same things can be said about some of the things you talk about.

John: How is that?

Q: When you say 'just notice that there is awareness', 'just look and see if you can find a separate 'I', or 'dismantle the beliefs and concepts that arise'—these things seem similar to what this teacher is saying. I admit that they are much more 'subtle' and do not feel as much like techniques.

John: It appears so, but there is a distinct difference, really. I never say that there is an individual who is present and needs to achieve something he does not have. The first and most important pointer is the suggestion to come back to the recognition that what you are seeking you already are. That presence-awareness is who you are now, fully and completely. I never suggest that there is something to do or achieve that is not already present. Nor do I prescribe any techniques or activities for the supposed individual to do per se. It is more a pointer to come back to an understanding of two basic points, which are—what you are (awareness) and what you are not (an assumed autonomous individual apart from this). It is an encouragement to look and understand the correct position. It is not taking the individual to be present and real and then giving him a set of techniques to do to get free.

There is a difference. It is not just a matter of one being more subtle, as if what I am saying is just a more subtle variation of dualism. It may appear that way due to the language. However, there is a radical difference in the consideration of the issue at a very fundamental level. One approach can strengthen or enhance the concept of separation. The other liquidates it. The proof is in the experience, not in the verbal formulations.

Q: But my question is, how can 'I' do any of these things?

John: You are stumbling, half-knowingly, into the heart of the matter. Ultimately, there is no 'I' or entity who needs to do anything or can do anything. Remember, the basic pointer is that you are that pure non-dual presence itself now, always and effortlessly. There is no separate individual at all. You have intuited this correctly. As I have said many times, the belief in separation is the root of all doubts, questions, seeking, suffering and so on. When all is oneness, what is there to do or seek or know? The game is up. What I can say is that if this (that is, no 'I') is seen deeply or recognized, there are no longer any questions or doubts to speak of. In short, we would not be having this conversation!

Q: Is not talking about this at all misleading if there is not an 'I' who is there to do any of these things?

John: Quite the contrary. In fact, for one who is interested in genuine understanding and lasting freedom such pointers are like music to the ears because they finally and fully expose the root of the matter. Upon looking into this, there are no real dilemmas or problems left and these questions are no longer raised. They are unnecessary. The fact of presence-awareness and the absence of separation are clear.

However, to an apparent individual plagued with questions, doubts, beliefs and the resultant confusion and suffering, the pointer is given to see his nature and attempt to find the imagined separate one. It appears to be given as a direction to the individual. However, note the word 'appears'. The one with the question or doubt is under the sway of the illusion of being a separate someone. So that apparent someone is encouraged to have a look and see what is true. Who is being directed? The imaginary separate someone still under the sway of that belief.

Does this accentuate the belief? Not at all. For it is bringing the very notion under scrutiny. Who is looking? The question is not really needed. There is no need to bring a supposed someone into the picture and then get back into the loop of doubts and questions generated by doing that. Just see if there is anything there other than presence-awareness. The seeing reveals the true position. Who sees? No one! It is just a natural recognition, not by a limited entity. It is just a movement of clear knowing of the fact that oneness is all there is. Far from being a dualistic technique that fosters or strengthens the concept of 'I' or separation, it pretty much annihilates it on the spot. This is a matter of experience, not just hypothesizing.

Another workable approach is simply to state outright that there is no entity and nothing except oneness. It is really a condensed version of the same pointer. If there is resonance with that, that is excellent. However, if it does not quite click, often times people are left waiting for 'something' to happen, especially if such concepts as 'awakening' or 'liberation' are subtly or inadvertently reinforced. I find the approach I am suggesting to be more emphatic and clear. But that is just my opinion! Each must find his own poison!

Q: It seems like either 'I' remember to notice presence or dismantle a belief or 'I' do not. Or more correctly, noticing and/or dismantling happen or they do not. There is not even an 'I' involved.

John: Correct. This is not done by someone, as you are seeing, because there is no one. However, there is just a natural intelligence, a natural resonance, an innate knowing that arises to investigate and see the truth. All thinking beings are innately interested in who and what they are. There is a natural curiosity that comes up to meet the pointers. There is no need to bring any entity into the picture in any of this. It is just as your eyes are seeing. There is no limited entity seeing. It is just seeing. In the same way, there is just a natural curiosity to see what is true.

Q: In my direct experience it seems that either awareness 'arises' and cuts off involvement with the 'story-line' or it does not.

John: Awareness neither rises nor sets. It is clear and ever-present. This is just pointed out. You can take a look and verify this if you like. Why not? It is not difficult and can be seen right now. There is no need to cut off any story-line. I am not sure where this idea came in. If you fight thoughts you are back in duality again.

Q: No matter how hard 'I' try to make that happen, it does not increase the frequency or duration of the awareness episodes.

John: This is because you are missing the simplicity of things. You are making a dualism where there need not be one. These are all concepts based on the notion that you are a limited someone who needs something to be free. But you are free, and the limited someone is not present. So have a look.

Q: I guess what I am saying is that it seems that no matter how clearly someone articulates this subject (and you do it very well indeed), any sort of understanding of this is not useful, because there is nothing 'I' can do with that understanding.

John: Of course! Because there is no 'I' present to do anything. However, there is in fact an understanding and recognition that arises that clarifies all of this quite well. All I can do is point to the obvious. The natural intelligence that you are will rise to follow the pointers naturally.

Q: And even experiences of 'seeing' are not helpful because there is nothing 'I' can do to bring them on. The obvious solution is to realize there is no 'I' and all the questions and 'trying' would disappear along with that. But once again, that seems like something that either happens or it does not.

John: Do not worry. Just look. That is all I can say. It sounds dualistic, but all I can say is it works wonderfully well.

Q: All of this ties me in mental knots (as I am sure it does a lot people). But it all comes down to whether or not there is such a thing as an individual doer. Even teachers who say there is not a doer still talk about things you can do (although they do not phrase it that way). If we really are not the doers, then reading or talking or noticing or feeling, and so on, are all meaningless. They will happen or not happen in spite of us.

John: Well, you still have the idea that something needs to happen, and that idea is stringing you along. See that concept as false. What you are looking for is clear and evident now as that sense of undeniable presence shining at your core. There is nothing to get at all. If you truly see that no one is there, all problems drop immediately. If there is no one there, who has problems? So your experience belies a residual belief in the presence of a separation. So, here it comes (!), have a look to see if it is true.

Q: Thanks for your work and your kind consideration, John.

John: Have a look and see if any of this helps or hinders! All I can say is it really does work quite well in practice. It is more workable to simply understand the pointers rather than debating about them. What are the basic pointers in a nutshell? Awareness, your real nature, is all there is. The imaginary self you have taken yourself to be does not exist. That is the final word.

Follow up ...

Q: I realize that the secret is in 'just looking'. Calling it a 'secret' is just a way of phrasing it. I know there is no secret at all. In fact, it is the most obvious thing in the world. In just looking, there is no problem at all. There is just a natural seeing of what is. What I was doing was attaching all sorts of concepts to the looking, complicating the whole issue by taking on ideas about it such as 'looking is a technique', 'who is the one looking?' 'I had better remember to look often today', 'when will the looking (seeing) become permanent?' and so on. By doing that, I was consistently missing the heart of the matter. It is the 'just' part of 'just looking' that is so important. There is no agenda, no assumptions about how, no assumptions about what should or should not be seen, no attempt to do anything about it, no hierarchy of things that are seen, no good or bad in what is seen. There is just the looking and just the seeing. Seeing is happening continually anyway. It is actually much harder and more stressful to not see (or believe you are not seeing) than it is to just see. Thank you, John.

John: You are onto something here!

77

Habits Are Just Ideas

Question: I just wanted to say hello and tell you it is a joy to read your articles. I have written to you before. I remember telling you last that 'I needed you once, but not anymore'. Well, maybe that is true or maybe it is not. It depends on when you ask me (and who I think you would be asking). I cannot sustain any questions, though. They all seem to pass as effortlessly as they come. Nothing is interesting but the joy, the clear, empty space of presence-awareness, always upstream, unmoving. The essence is just 'be still', 'be quiet'. How many ways can this be expressed? And how many ways is it ignored? But the thirty-to-forty year old habits die hard, apparently! Anyway, thanks again, so much.

John: Thanks for the note. As far as I can see, you are on your way with all this. If no serious doubts are arising, there is no need to tamper with things. Presence-awareness is solid and clear at all times, as is your identity as that. It is clear, open, spacious and serene by nature. This is your nature. All else is only a thought or concept appearing like a lone cloud in the infinite sky of space-like awareness.

Habits are just ideas arising. Even the concept of 'thirty-to-forty years' is arising as a present notion. From the point of view of awareness, which is the true perspective, there is no time at all. As usual, believing false ideas to be true puts the focus on the unreal and we overlook the clear and obvious. No harm. We never move away from being-awareness. This is pointed out and the truth of it dawns. Is the dawning sudden or gradual? Neither, for time is a concept arising in present awareness. That is clear and evident, and you are that.

78

Dismantling, Shifting Gears and Flatness

Question: You are quite ruthless in discriminating between what is and what is not. It is precisely what is required. Thank you. The story line I have followed all my life is now dismantling. I see I was only fuelling it with my mind, for want of a better word. And now the sense of myself as an individual is so undercut, as are notions of a past and a future, that I cannot sustain a sense of a story any longer.

John: This is what happens when you wade into all this! This is good because, as you know, the story is the story of a fictional character, that is, the 'me' we have taken ourselves to be.

Q: Nonetheless, a story does still seem to present itself.

John: It is just an appearance, a flow of events patterning in awareness. A story is for a character. With no entity present there is not really a story, so much as an unfolding or flowering of life. What kind of story there is is highly provisional and not taken seriously. It is not about 'you', so all the concern dissipates.

Q: The apparent story is not linear, but rather it seems to be a succession of quiet explosions on a static screen. But it is not a mind-driven story. Rather, it is something which unfolds just because it can.

John: Yes, just a moment-to-moment arising. It is all very effortless and not a problem.

Q: And yet as that linear sense of the story dismantles, there seems to be some sadness, some grief, some flatness, even some sense of loss. It is like coming across a treasured doll from childhood and not feeling the same love and affection for her. It is like that is how I feel about 'myself'. I was such a heroine in my story! And now the heroine is empty, and there is no story! There is flatness. And I guess I should realize that this flatness is also it.

John: We have been so used to looking to the appearance and to the story for our support that when it starts to dismantle, there can be a bit of loss, as if the ground is giving way. This is because of the residual habit of looking at the appearance. But the presence-awareness that you are is full of light, clarity, presence, intelligence and endless possibilities. It is the 'intelligence-energy' animating it all. As the recognition settles in with this, those attributes, if you will, are recognized.

Q: I should perhaps explain that when I discovered non-duality six months ago, I had to walk away from a hell of a lot. I was involved in a whole spiritual practice in which I had friends, a direction and a purpose. I even had a starring role, editing books for the director. But when non-duality clicked, I had to walk away from it all.

John: When all the belief structures are undercut, we may not have the same interest in things as we did before, and there may be a bit of reshuffling.

Q: So it seems as though this flatness is just arising. I mention it because I was a bit disconcerted to read in 'Shining In Plain View' that joy is a sign of this awareness. There is very little joy right now, just this flatness. I wondered if you could cast any light on this experience?

John: The awareness seems almost quality-less from the point of view of the mind. You could say that it appears as a nothing. Objectively, it is a nothingness. However, in and of itself (yourself), it is bright, open, clear and full of immense richness and depth. Just abide with the recognition that you are that constant presence of awareness illumining all, even the appearance of flatness in the mind. When you look in this way, you will see the depth of it. As Nisargadatta Maharaj once said, 'My silence sings; my emptiness is full'.

Q: But is not the flatness also it?

John: I have a different take on it. I would say the flatness appears in it. Do not overlook what is bright, clear and full of life in you. Awareness is not limited by any experience that is arising, even if it be a sense of flatness.

Q: But I have to say this feels almost like a period of shifting gears. It is almost as though I am grieving for the search for enlightenment. It had gone on for so many years. Yet as I write, I see I cannot even take refuge in that. Who is there here to grieve?

John: You will come to see that search for enlightenment was nothing but pure misery. It was looking away from an answer that was always present, your natural being. It is so evident and clear that it needs no realization at all. And this is what the genuine teachers had been pointing to all along. However, there can be a bit of readjustment to the new view. Everything comes to balance naturally.

Q: I think I also have to say that in addition to this flatness, I also experience some panic on occasion! As just then when I was writing that last sentence, I realized that there is truly no refuge. There is only awareness. There is no one to blame, nowhere to hide. There is only this, and I find that quite scary. Do others experience this?

John: This just a residual habit reaction. It will settle down as you realize that the awareness within you, which is what you are, remains steady and clear at all times. The fear and panic were born in not recognizing this. Some old habits and concepts may pop up. Just see them for what they are—residual notions picked up in the years of ignorance. Nothing can shake you from your clear and present nature. The recognition of this ushers in a life of clarity and joy. You will see this in experience as you let all this resonate and settle in.

Q: As usual, I am grateful for whatever response you are able to provide. I do not want to get too wordy about this, but as I read your words yesterday, I felt this apparent expansion. Yes, I know! An experience! But there is something behind the words that is somehow transmitted or resounds deeply. In short, I am deeply appreciative. Many thanks for all your help and for the books. They are just great.

John: Keep in touch. I am glad to hear things are resonating. It is your innate knowing resonating with this. All the words are just pointers to what you are. Follow the pointers and come back to the recognition of what is clear and present in you. Then you do not need pointers any longer. You do not need any pointers or teachings to be what you are.

Consciousness Is Beyond Doubt

Question: I have been reading quite a lot of this type of stuff recently. I even thought I 'got it' for a day or two!

John: The most important thing is to first find out what 'it' is. Until then, we are more or less grasping at straws, because we may not be precisely clear on what is being pointed to.

Q: But I am not quite there yet (wherever that might be!).

John: Again, to define what it is we are looking for allows these questions to come to clarity. What is 'it'? Where is 'it'? Where is 'there'? These are basic questions to get you started!

Q: Based on my background, I do know that while science and rational thinking are very good ways to investigate the apparent rules of the game, they can never actually explain why there is a game in the first place.

John: The mind is an appearance within the manifestation, a part of the whole. We are probing into the source of the appearance. The mind, in the end, is completely incapable of understanding this. The part cannot grasp the whole. The mind cannot understand what is beyond the mind. In other words, the answer is not in the mind.

Q: It seems there can be no answer to the ultimate questions such as 'Why?' and 'For what purpose do we exist?' and so on.

John: In my view this is correct. 'Why?' is just another formulation by the mind to grasp what is beyond its ken. The question 'why?' assumes time, causality and purpose. All of those things are fine for things in the appearance or within the mind's field of inquiry. But what is being pointed to (that timeless presence beyond the mind) is not subject to time, space, purpose, causality and so on. In others words, the 'why?' does not ultimately apply to what is being pointed to.

To cut to the chase—what is pointed to is the sense of existence, which is also aware, in you. That is actually vividly present, yet utterly non-objective and non-conceptual. Thoughts, perceptions and sensations arise within that. Time, space, causality, bodies, worlds and all else are fabricated or constructed within awareness. But awareness stands beyond, 'upstream' of the content. Thus it is timeless, spaceless, causeless and non-dual. It needs no reason to be. It is. All else appears. That which appears is not ultimately real. The mind deals with appearances, not reality. To know what is real, you must look beyond the mind to that changeless knowing principle within yourself that illumines thoughts, feelings and sensations. It is not difficult, because it is self-evident and shining in plain view at all times as that principle to which the words 'I am' point. It is your true being. Everything gets back to the recognition and understanding of this.

Q: All there has ever been as far as first-hand experience goes is (my) consciousness, my existence, my reality. That is my direct experience. Before I was born there was nothing.

John: Here you are assuming your identity to be the body. The body is just an appearance in awareness. You are the awareness. The birth and death of the body are not your birth and death. You say before the birth of the body there was nothing. How do you know? This is a supposition, a guess. It is a concept appearing now in awareness.

Even now, awareness appears as 'no thing' to the mind, because it is non-objective. That no-thing-ness is with you right now as the clear awareness. The changes of the body-mind do not change that. Seeing this, there is no longer concern about the coming and going of the body.

Q: When I die I am guessing there will be exactly the same nothing.

John: Yes. The same 'no thing', which is the presence-awareness that you are. Bodies come and go, but life, awareness, being remain. Billions and billions of bodies come and go, yet the fact of being remains. You are that being-ness that remains in spite of the changing appearances.

Q: With respect to free will, at best, it is very, very limited. At worst, there is no free will at all.

John: Free will is a notion pertaining to an individual entity who is presumed to have it or not. Deep investigation reveals the individual is a fiction. So the whole discussion is moot. That is why the age-long debate has never been conclusively resolved. The basic issue, that there is no individual present, has been largely overlooked. In practice, thoughts, events, decisions, preferences and all the rest simply appear spontaneously.

Q: I must admit that I am quite happy with the fact that I have got the starring role in my own existence!

John: You may think so—until you investigate and discover that the person you have taken yourself to be is not present! The character we take ourself to be is a fiction, an assumption. And that is the root of the metaphysical dilemma. This was

Buddha's key insight centuries ago. His recognition of this led him to the end of suffering and doubts. So the story goes.

Q: Everything takes place in my consciousness. That is true. In fact, it might be the case that the whole ball game is just one big illusion of sorts. It might be that no one or nothing exists except in my consciousness, whatever that is. This is sometimes called nihilism isn't it!?

John: This is a key insight. Everything is a movement in conscious. The status or reality of what appears is open to speculation. However, the fact of consciousness is not doubtable. This is why the exploration of consciousness is the only path to complete certitude. Consciousness is the only thing (if you can call it a thing) that is utterly beyond doubt.

Q: Well, I behave as if there is a real world out there! I follow the apparent rules that need to be followed. I do not just jump off a cliff to test out my theory!

John: The reality of the external world is a working hypothesis. It is adequate for daily living, just like when we are in a dream we more or less take it at face value. But in exploring things from an ultimate perspective, we ought not take anything at all for granted.

Q: I still seem to own my existence. I do not particularly want to or not want to. It just seems to be, in the sense that if you and I sat down and compared notes on our versions of reality, we would find they are different. I would have my version, and you would have your version. This is my direct experience. This seems to be the way the game is.

John: Different body-mind instruments in the appearance

have differing perspectives, just like two cameras placed in different locations record different scenes. What is the problem?

Q: The bottom line is I still seem to want to believe in my existence rather than just existence. And I guess, because of that, I still have to question non-duality or oneness or whatever words we might like to call it.

John: Start with the fact that your actual being is present and beyond doubt. Without that, what else can you have? That being is both present and aware. Everything that you can possibly know is an appearance in and on that. This is completely water-tight. In direct evidence, there is no knowledge of anything that is not arising as an appearance in this that you are. Even the ideas 'my', 'oneness' and so on are just concepts appearing in awareness. Are you with me?

Now, the appearances are pretty much an insubstantial flux with no real lasting reality. So if there is something true or lasting, it is not going to be there. That leaves your being-awareness as the likely possibility to explore. I will give a clue and say that essence lies in the non-conceptual recognition of your true nature. You cannot think your way into this because the mind invariably deals with objects and your being is not an object.

Once you have seen all this, the mind can be left behind. To know who you are or to recognize your true nature is not difficult. It is that simple sense of presence-awareness that is with you right now. It is effortlessly present and shining in plain view at all times. We have just overlooked it because we did not know where to look.

Q: I do admit that there is something that resonates in this stuff for me.

John: Well, you are on the trail back to the recognition to your true self. Perhaps some of these pointers will strike a chord.
Q: Perhaps you can help put me out of my misery!

John: The best way to be put out of your misery is to find out what you are and let go of what you are not. The supposed 'me' that we think we are is an assumption. It is not truly present. To look for and discover its absence annihilates it on the spot.

Where Is the Evidence for Awareness?

Question: I can easily focus on sight when seeing something or hearing when hearing something, but to be aware of one central awareness of everything is more difficult.

John: Not only is it difficult, it is impossible! You cannot be aware of awareness because you are awareness. It is so evident that we overlook the obvious. Even though awareness is singular and non-objective, it is well-known and clear at all times. You could say that it is self-knowing.

Q: It can feel like there is no evidence of one awareness, only awareness of things. Until awareness-of-all is found, where is the evidence for it?

John: Because, if I ask you if you are aware, you instinctively and automatically say 'yes' without any effort. It is an obvious fact. Without being aware you could have no experience of anything else at all. An object does not perceive itself. It is known by you.

Q: Can awareness exist without something that it is aware of? How can the answer be experienced?

John: Because awareness knows both the presence and absence of what appears. In any given moment a flood of thoughts and sensations is coming and going. Yet the fact of being present and aware remains clear. Otherwise, how can you speak of the passing experiences?

Q: A pointer that resonated with me recently was to see what is closer to me than the sensations and appearances.

John: Yes, this is a good one!

Q: However, it seems as if I need to scoop up all of the appearances before looking away from them. I need to observe everything in my experience before retracting away from it and abiding as what it all arises in. Was this your experience?

John: No. You are making it too complicated. You are present and aware, yes? Awareness is. You are that which is aware. That is all. There is no need to turn it into a practice or attainment. Otherwise, you are back in the mind and looking away from the obvious.

Q: Remaining as awareness only seems to take considerable effort, making sure that nothing but awareness is included in the practice.

John: No. Remaining as awareness is effortless because it is what you are. It is not a practice, but a recognition of an ever-present fact.

Q: For me, this requires constant correction as I realize I am taking myself to be more than just awareness. Of course, the effort itself is also another appearance and not 'my' effort, necessary though it seems. Is this just another distraction?

John: You may remind yourself for a time that you are awareness, but each time you check, there you are—present and aware. After a while, the looking falls away because you see that it is just the natural state of affairs.

However, to discriminate between your true nature as awareness and the appearances you have falsely taken yourself to be is good. It just helps to clarify the true position. But there is no need to practice to be what you are. Just clarify the true position to your satisfaction. Avoid making this a practice, as that tends to accentuate the old belief in being separate and limited, an entity who needs to get something. You are none of those. Being-awareness is what is real, and you are that. You do not become that. You are that.

81

The Core Insights

Question: You say that things became clear to you only after your teacher pointed them out. I have been reading correspondence on your site. There is a distinct resonance, a feeling of peace. Now I am waiting for the penny to drop about the nonexistence of a separate self. Is there something I can do to hasten it, though I know you frown on practice? As of now, I do a bit of meditation first thing in the morning and read stuff from your site and other sites on this perspective.

John: Here is the short course! Being-awareness is what you are. It is the simple and inescapable fact of being present and aware. This is the core insight. You are that fully and completely now. If there is any doubt, look into this until it is utterly clear.

The appearance consists of thoughts, feelings and sensations flickering through awareness. None of those lasts. None of them has any substantial or independent existence. None of those constitute who you are. There is no entity, person or 'I' in those things at all.

Suffering is self-centered thoughts, that is, thoughts that reference a person who is supposed to have or own those thoughts. Yet that person is not findable. None of the thoughts, feelings or sensations constitute who you are. So, you, as a presumed defective, separate person are not actually observable or findable. We say 'I am no good' or 'I am not free' or whatever. But who or what is this 'I'? Have we ever found or seen such a thing in the picture?

In short, try to find any evidence of something that you are prepared to take hold of and a say 'this is me'. This is a way to get started with this. Remember, even though you cannot find any such thing as a person or substantial self, you cannot deny the fact of your true being which is the 'cognizing emptiness' which everything appears within or on.

82

The Waiting Game

Question: It seems that the pointers are understood and that all questions drop away, but ...

John: The notorious 'but'! As you may have noticed, questions, problems and doubts are generated in thought. They arise in response to a fundamental doubt about our true nature. They are really the mind's attempts to come to grips with the fundamental question of identity. Stepping back for a moment, you can see that being or awareness is simply that knowing space of presence that is constantly illumining all thoughts, feelings and sensations. It is much like the sun radiating pure light on whatever is passing beneath. As the sun is not affected by the clouds passing through the sky, so awareness is not affected by the arising and passing of content in it. It is vivid, clear, bright, luminous, radiant, alive and spacious at all times. Your being as presence-awareness is completely beyond doubt.

As I say, thoughts, feelings and sensations arise in awareness. Ultimately, they are nothing but that awareness, because they have no independent existence apart from it. The mere arising of those things is not a problem. It is all arising and passing in the space of vivid clarity and presence. This is especially clear when you see that all appearances are shining right in the luminous presence of awareness that you are. So there is no problem at all. Finished!

But doubts and questions do seem to arise. The mind drifts into confusion, doubt, questions, imagined problems and so on, and the clear recognition of our true nature seems to diminish. Why? It is simply a non-recognition of the principle of awareness. With that non-recognition arises the belief that we exist as something apart, something limited, fragmented, isolated, alone. This is the root notion of separation. From that assumption, the mind generates a flow of thinking concerned with that seeming separate one. Those thoughts are something like a cloud of images held together by ignorance and blind belief. They do not obscure the true position, yet there can be a fixation on them, which is all that suffering really is—the fixation on or belief in erroneous ideas, which are, in turn, driven by the assumption that we have separated from oneness. Of course we have not, so a little bit of investigation restores the true position (that was never really lost). With that comes the recognition of the innate clarity and spaciousness of your essence. That is the whole pointing in a nutshell.

All questions, moods, states and so on are experiences in awareness. They come and go based on the causes and conditions within the mind. They are mostly driven by beliefs, concepts and attitudes held in the mind. A combination of focus on the mind, belief in separation and belief in self-centered concepts as true is what keeps the mechanism rolling. There is no harm, ultimately, and the intrinsic awareness is never compromised at all. In any moment, the recognition of what is true and clear in you restores clarity, which of course has not disappeared, but is overlooked. Once this is seen, it becomes apparent that clarity, in fact, is ever-present, and the belief in the separate person and all of its self-centered notions that we used to take for real are exposed. They are no longer a factor driving the flow of conceptual thinking.

Q: Somehow I still feel there is some kind of waiting game, as if something is supposed to happen.

John: Well, there may still be some kind of residual belief that there is something to get in order to reach happiness or freedom. There is not, because your innate being of presence-awareness is all there is. It is the source of all and the source of joy itself. So the waiting game is based on an erroneous concept. The future does not exist, except in imagination. It is a mirage. The waiting game is looking away from the source of clarity and looking into a future which is non-existent. See this concept as false. In this seeing, the concept drops away naturally and you abide as the natural and innate clarity that you are.

Q: There is something in the mind resisting this so ordinary life.

John: There is no ordinary life. Life is a grand display or flowering within the vast and clear presence of the divine intelligence. Every leaf and piece of dust is cradled in an expanse of light and presence. That presence-awareness that contains all things is also the deep presence of love and peace always. It is your own real being. The universe being revealed in each moment is aflame with the presence of exquisite love. In that, even the most ordinary thing is a unique and wonderful expression of the underlying oneness of all.

Q: One teacher speaks about falling in love with this, that all this is a love affair, that you come back to the innocence of a little child and so on. But for me, there is just some flatness, sometimes boredom. There is also sometimes an ease, but nothing such as blissfulness or love or anything extraordinary.

John: Once the attention comes off the mind-created concepts and returns to the non-conceptual recognition of actual presence-awareness, you discover a clarity and joy there that is unmistakable. It is shining now, but we are tending to look back to the mind and its states instead of just relaxing with the recognition of the natural presence of clarity. That is not dependent on mind states. All the states, boring or not boring, may continue but there is a dawning recognition of the light shining behind them so to speak.

Q: I know that all the concepts are crap, but there is still this subtle waiting game for more than just this. From your experience, could you elaborate a bit on this?

John: This, meaning your real being of presence-awareness, is full to the brim of clarity and joy. Just be willing to be with that and let it reveal its depths. This does not contradict the natural ebb and flow of body and mind states, which will continue to fluctuate based on conditions and circumstances. However, you will catch the fragrance of a certain ease and clarity as the recognition of presence-awareness as your nature reveals itself. Nothing is brought in. Nothing is changed. It is a simple recognition of something so clear that we just overlooked it until now.

Follow up ...

Q: Thank you. When you say things like 'aflame with the presence of exquisite love'—that is what creates the trouble and the feeling of separation ...

John: It is just a poetic description of who you are. Awareness is not a flat, bland thing. It is alive, vital, radiant, clear and immensely full of joy. That is why the Hindus call your real nature 'sat-chit-ananda'. To point to it brings in no separation. How could it? It is simply pointing to the undeniable presence-awareness that you are. Give up the fixation on words and simply abide in and as the non-conceptual presence-awareness that you are. At this point, further discussion and thinking is useless because it leads back into the mind, words and concepts. A word is not the thing, and you are not a word. Better give up while you are ahead!

Q: That kind of talk makes it seem like 'you' see something 'I' cannot see.

John: Here is where the problem comes in. There is no 'you' or 'I' at all, only the one presence-awareness shining in all directions. If you pick up the belief of 'you' and 'I', then separation and duality starts. So do not do it, and all is fine as is.

Q: Still, like that other teacher with his 'love affair', it sounds very good, but it can be very misleading. I cannot fall in love with this, so I do not get it!

John: There is nothing to get. You are what you are seeking. Furthermore, there is no 'I' present to get anything. A slight residual belief in those concepts keeps you spinning. Seeing this, the whole mechanism falls to pieces.

Q: There is only awareness, so love or no love—who cares?

John: You seem to! For the record, your concept of awareness seems a bit pale and flat. From here, and in fact, awareness is that timeless presence illuminating all of creation, the changeless ground of being from which everything rises and into which it sets, inseparable from the heart of love itself. Why not take a dive into it and see exactly what this presence-awareness that you are really is? This is not advocating separation, but just a suggestion to get to know what you already are.

83

The Fact of Your Being Is Never Doubtful

Question: I am looking for personal serenity and 'the truth'. The truth, to my mind, is a model of reality that correctly predicts all known events, phenomena, and so on. This means, of course, that the truth might actually change. This sounds contradictory, but it is not, so long as one realizes that all we can ever know is the current nearest approximation to a perhaps non-existent ultimate truth. Does that make sense?

John: This may be so at the level of the mind and appearances, where all knowing is relative and provisional. But when it comes to the knowledge of your self, you arrive at a much greater degree of certitude. This is because what you are investigating is your self. Your own being-awareness is present and beyond doubt, as is your identity as that. Your own being is the one and only thing that you can know with certainty. The fact of your being is never doubtful.

Q: One question that seems to be arising for me is—is the mind in awareness, or is awareness in the mind? My core personal experience is that the mind is in awareness. But still it is my awareness, in the sense it is different from yours. My 'high school science' mind is saying that consciousness is formed inside the brain, a product of neurons doing their business. But I have to say that my personal experience is that the mind turned up after awareness. First there was awareness. Then a concept of mind appeared in awareness, as did a concept of 'I'. There was a time that I was aware and there was no 'I' at all. It is time to reach for the headache tablets!

As for me, what am I? The best I can come up with is that

I am a concept in my own awareness. If I talk about me, there is some idea of body, thought patterns, typical behavior and so on. I guess the next question is, 'Is that really me?' In some sense I guess it is not. At the core of me, without the abstractions and concepts, is a stream of consciousness. Subjectively, that is all there has ever been.

One issue for me is that a term like 'oneness' seems to imply that we are all the same thing. But if we all have our own subjective existence, we are not one, are we? That is probably not very clear, but perhaps you can glimpse the question that is forming? I am actually happy with the concept that all I know is my reality, my awareness. Or perhaps I am 'an' awareness, the only one I know. But still I have got a hang up with the feeling that your awareness is different from mine.

John: Awareness, the fact of being present and aware, is the key entry point in this approach. Now, everything that appears or can be known, including the body, senses, mind and world, arises because it appears or is registered in awareness. Although awareness doubtlessly exists (otherwise, how could we be cognizant of anything?), it does not stand out in front of us as a thing or object to be perceived. It is the knower, not the known. The known, by definition, is an arising in awareness. This is what makes awareness appear to be mysterious. It is undoubtedly present, but in and of itself, it is not a thing that can be perceived, sensed or thought about directly. Yet, intuitively, or non-conceptually, there is a clear recognition of what is being pointed to.

Awareness, as awareness, is not definable as mine or yours. Those are both ideas arising in the awareness. In other words, the mind, which is appearing in awareness, creates the concepts of 'me' and 'you' and then tries to label awareness or limit it by those definitions.

Time arises in awareness. Space arises in awareness. The world, body, mind, concepts, notions, ideas, questions and so on all arise in awareness. But awareness is not bound by the appearances in it. It is not in time. It is eternal (that is, external—out of time). Space, causality, purpose, duality and all other categories also arise as objects in awareness. Awareness is not subject to time, causality, purpose and so on. Also, birth and death apply to objects in awareness, but not awareness itself. This awareness is what you are. All the high falutin' descriptions of awareness are descriptions of your real nature. You are timeless, birthless, deathless, causeless and so on. The coming and going of appearances does not touch your real essence at all.

The idea of being a limited, separate self is a concept created in the mind, which we have falsely taken as true. And this is the root of the metaphysical problem. To correct this false conceptual framework through exposing it as false restores the true view and ushers in genuine self-knowledge.

All that appears manifests from and upon awareness. It is inseparable from awareness. In the last analysis, it is awareness. That is why to know your real nature as that awareness is described as oneness or non-duality. It is coming into recognition of the one essence or substance of which everything is an expression. Oneness means no separation, no duality, no limitation, no fear. That is why this recognition is synonymous with deep peace, the ending of fear and so on. It is actually a positive experience of contentment, peace, wholeness and fulfillment. Hindus called it 'ananda', which is happiness or deep peace.

This is why your real nature is described as 'existence-awareness-happiness'. It is one essence described in three different ways. From the point of view of the appearances, it is that unchanging sense of existence. From the point of view of the mind, it is that constant light of knowing that is registering the arising and setting of thoughts. From the point of view of feelings or the heart, it is that feeling of oneness or unity, which is happiness, peace or love.

84

Noticing Peace or Joy Is Not Difficult

Question: I could say I am excited beyond belief by our meeting yesterday, but delighted is a better word. I did not immediately ponder what I had learned, but just went about the usual things that I do. Actually, I went shopping! Perhaps that is better than trying to be too studious about our subject. It does not mean I am not going to digest or percolate yesterday's discoveries.

Somehow, what we discussed about the person really hit home, and I finally understood that I do not need a mystical experience of 'the self falling away' in order to know that I am not this character in a melodramatic novel that I continually write in my head. Prior to our meeting, I had been thinking about the fact that what I usually think of as the self, that is to say, the body, has needs that must be met. But it is not me. And the thoughts and self-images, all the history, the intrigues, the drama (like my belief that some people hate or dislike me) is not me. They are only words and images.

My true nature is peace, freedom, and joy—at least I have held that as an ideal over the years. I have intuitively felt that I might as well believe in my self, in the greater Self. Yet I did not realize that I do not even have to do that, at least not as some kind of strident effort.

Over the course of attending your sessions on non-duality, I have been chipping away at my lifelong 'expectations' habit, of thinking the realization is going to be a total change and that it will be in the future. I told you yesterday how I had expected all this peace and joy to flood my being instantly, and how that expectation was blocking my actual experience of peace and joy. We have talked about this before, but it became clearer to me that noticing peace or joy is not a difficult thing or something I have to try to do. It is about noticing, not straining.

I know that 'the natural state' is not something you can give me. At the same time, I feel that talking with you and noticing your complete conviction and ease with this truth, as well as your loving kindness and ease with your own being and with other people, has been immeasurably helpful in demonstrating this truth in action, in the flesh, in person. It is almost as if I imbibe or absorb it—not that 'it' is not on my side of the semi-permeable membrane. You have said too that spirituality is caught, not taught, and you have said the words do not matter a damn. It is in the sharing.

Perhaps it is this 'catching' of the truth that some are trying to demonstrate with their 'energy transfers'. Yet, we are all the energy. Even saying that this energy can be transferred is misleading. When I followed that path, it seemed very frustrating not to feel changed by the energy-givers' most strenuous efforts, as if I were a very hard case indeed.

Well, I am beginning to feel the way you talk about so often, that I am resonating with the pointers. What was that phrase Bob Adamson used? 'An energy will light up your face, a radiance, if you will ..'. or some such words. It makes me want to use fine words to construct, or at least recall, beautiful webs of thought to make 'the Word flesh', to dwell among us, and to show 'His glory, the glory as of the only-begotten of the Father, full of truth and light', (Gospel of St. John), 'the light that never was on land or sea' (Milton, I think). Thank you for sharing with me.

John: Thank you for sharing your insights and comments. You write and express yourself very well. I do not have much to add, just to say that, as you are doing, it is good to keep things simple and watch how the pointers apply in your own direct experience. Things are unfolding beautifully. It is your own resonance and interest that brings you back to consider what is clear and present in you.

85

Discover That in You Which Never Leaves

Question: I have been enjoying reading the articles on your site and really love the style you use to point to our true nature. I was reading some of your responses to peoples e-mails and then for about one minute I saw something I had been overlooking the whole time—my true self. There were no thoughts going through my head, but there was a realization saying 'I know you, you have been there all the time, but I just got you confused with the thoughts in my head'. It was as if in that moment I stepped back from the thoughts and could see them from a distance and they were just objects that did not have anything to do with me at all. It was as if nothing had changed, yet everything had changed at the same time.

John: This is very good and clearly stated. This is the essence of it right there.

Q: This lasted for about an hour. Then I was back into the thoughts. The mind wanted to own the experience. It wanted to analyze it and tell everyone about it.

John: This is all just a movement of thoughts and concepts. If you do not attach to them and give them much belief, they sail right through and leave you as you always are—present and aware.

Q: And now, a week later, I am feeling as if it never happened.

John: But did you stop being present and aware? Do not

overlook that in you that was originally recognized to be true! Do not trade that recognition for the belief in a bunch of mind-created concepts built on a supposedly limited sense of self. That is all that is happening.

Q: I am able to be in awareness (sorry, I know that language is going to trip me up here) and the thoughts will go by without much attachment. But it is the physical, bodily feelings that do not seem to dissipate.

John: These will settle down naturally as the basic recognition of your real essence stabilizes. Keep in mind that this is not about making experiences go away, but rather discovering that in you which never leaves! With that recognition, everything comes to balance just fine.

Q: I have a lot of anxiety about my home life. I have neighbors who are very noisy, and everyday I am anxious about whether there is going to be noise when I get home and if I am going to have to go and confront them about it or not. I have this knot in my stomach all the time.

John: Physical sensations are usually based on feelings. Feelings in turn are based on thoughts, beliefs and attitudes. These depend on our view of ourselves. From my own experience, it is good to start with getting clear about your real nature. When the view of yourself is clear, the concepts and beliefs will not hang you up. Then the feelings will come into balance, along with the physical expressions. Life will find its natural expression.

Q: If you could give me a pointer or two, I would be most grateful.

John: See how those do.

You Are Effortlessly Present and Aware

Question: I just wanted to write to say how much I have gained (or lost—ha!) from reading the articles and writings on your site. I have been searching for many years, ever since being introduced to 'What Am I?' and 'The Overself' by a man who had been to India and through reading a lot of Paul Brunton's books. I also compiled a mass of books, tapes, videos, web sites—you name it—over the many, many years (about fifty!). Somehow, your direct, no nonsense responses (like Nathan Gill's and Ramana Maharshi's) have cut straight through to the core of it all, and I find myself entering that 'real me' when I read your writings.

John: Excellent. Just as a subtle point, once the basics are clear, and they are becoming so for you, there is no need to talk of yourself as entering the 'real me' or that such a thing happens on reading my writings. At a practical level, I appreciate what you are saying, but we might as well be clear as crystal on this. You are. You are fully existent and fully aware now. That being-awareness, or presence-awareness, is your true nature at this moment. It always was and always will be. It is not an attainment or an experience. It is not something you enter into and exit from. This is a radical and direct pointing to the fact of your nature—here and now—as the reality itself. The idea that 'I enter it' is a concept or belief that is arising in the very awareness that is your true, unchanging essence. Once the notion that 'I enter it' is subtly believed, then the opposite notion 'I exit it' comes in as a natural corollary. That is the way the opposites work. These thoughts and notions keep us looking away from the simplicity and availability of what is being pointed to. Just see that you cannot even have those ideas if you were not present and aware. That presence-awareness is what you are. It is not an attainment.

Q: As with Gill, you keep the focus on our real identity instead of all the various issues of a separate person we assume we are. Whew! It is so clear, clean and simple to be told over and over exactly what we are so that the habitual conviction of our separate individuality/ego is undermined, while our real identity is exposed again and again.

John: Yes! This is how it got pointed out to me, and I am grateful for the pointing that was direct, clear and simple. That is why I value that approach and keep to it as consistently as I can.

Q: Even though I have studied and learned all about the real me or Self, the jump into realizing has been weak and intermittent.

John: If you give reality to ideas like 'real me or Self' (versus your 'normal' self?), the need to jump into realization and so on, you will subtly be following the mind and overlooking the clear, present and obvious. It is the following of conceptual beliefs and taking them to be true that seemingly obscures the recognition of what is true and clear in you. However, it is not really possible for your real nature to be obscured. The recognition that our present being-awareness is what is real undercuts the belief in the erroneous concepts we have held about ourselves. This leaves you with the recognition that you are effortlessly present and aware and that this presence-awareness is your unchanging and continuous identity. You are already what you have been seeking. A little investigation clears this up straight away. You are not a limited, separate entity in need of anything, not even realization.

We falsely imagined we were and went in search of realizations and other fixes. But coming back to the recognition of our natural state, all those concepts are undercut and they are no longer needed and taken as true. Presence-awareness, which is what you are, is the reality itself. It needs no attainment or realization. It is the simple and undeniable fact of being, which is always beyond doubt.

Q: Somehow, the way you express it literally puts me there, at least for a moment, and it seems easier to return to the real with your teachings. So, once again, thank you for sharing these insights and pointers.

John: I am glad the pointers have had an impact and there has been a resonance. Now, pierce through any remaining concept of separation from the natural state. The effortless sense of being-awareness is what you are. Embrace that understanding now, not as a special attainment but as the recognition of an inescapable fact. You are both present and aware. That very presence-awareness is what you are, even now. The separation from that never occurred, except as a concept. That very concept could only arise right in this undeniable awareness itself. So the separation never actually happened. Seeing this, you stand naturally and effortlessly in the natural state of freedom and peace.

87

Begin To Explore This True Nature

Question: I had a particular event happen this past weekend that is currently causing a lot of commentary from my mind to flood whatever clarity I was experiencing in prior weeks. The power of the mind to affect us is amazing. I can sit and tell myself that to listen to the mind is nonsense and that it is not real. But even that line of thought is coming from the mind and thus does not work to push the commentary aside. I feel as if having someone help bring me back or make me aware of my true state might be particularly pertinent. I appreciate your time and thoughts.

John: Thanks for the note. What I found the best approach for me was to begin to understand a couple of basic points.

There is a natural sense of being or awareness that is constantly with us and without which nothing else can appear. Looking directly at this, which is really who and what we are, there is a dawning recognition of a deeper presence or source that is steady and clear, in spite of fluctuating thoughts and circumstances. It is something like a steady anchor point. Ultimately, the clear and direct knowing of what we are is where the clarity and freedom comes from. Not knowing this, we have imagined ourselves to be something that we are not, something limited and separate. All the other concepts and ideas flow from this. So, one way or another, to begin to explore this true nature that we are is important.

To go along with this, you can begin to appreciate that all of our doubts and sufferings are arisings in the mind. We take them to be true and give them a lot of interest. This is because we believe they say things that are real and significant about who we are. However, in focusing on these thoughts, we look away from the natural source of clarity and joy that is available. It is no use to try to push away thoughts. That is just more thoughts! It is more effective to just have a look and begin to see and understand what is happening. It is the understanding that is so liberating. See that the thoughts are fed and sustained by the belief that we are limited and separate and in need of something to be whole and complete. That is what the mind says, because it does not know any better. But we need to have a look and question to see if this is true. You will come to see that even when thoughts and concepts arise, they are doing so right in the awareness that you are. The very source of the clarity is shining right in the midst of the suffering thoughts. We are looking at the thoughts and not seeing the essence of what is true and real. So, the attention can come off the thoughts to recognize and appreciate the presence of your real nature.

Looking as above is a direct movement in the direction of a clear knowing of who you are. This has the effect of revealing a felt and lived sense of clarity. This undercuts the excessive focus on thought, which is the only thing that keeps us from seeing the clarity and freedom that is shining within us at all times.

Wordlessly Amazed

Questioner: Thank you very much, once again, for the generosity of your responses, John. I must apologize for having taken so long to get back to you. I have had a very busy couple of weeks. Oddly, in spite of not being able to give any attention to anything, there has been a continuous emergence of realizations. I cannot put it any better than this. Having spent many decades feeling that I have to put in a lot of spiritual spade work to get anywhere, as it were, with lots of meditation and vegetarianism and clean living, it is surprising to discover that there is indeed nothing to do. Just reading your website, books and generous responses to my e-mails is a bit like taking a pill. The magic seems to work without any attention. It is as though something is deeply recognized, and I am knowing from the inside out not the outside in. Does that make sense?

Usually, knowing or understanding comes from things being explained (from the outside). Now it is as though inner knowing, which is always there, is sort of exerting itself in my awareness, and as a result false understanding is ousted. I will literally stop in the middle of doing something (as now) and say 'Oh yes!' as I realize something that I already knew.

I have been so accustomed to seeing all this as a theory, as something that others know who are better informed than I, that it is a shock to suddenly stop in my tracks and realize, deeply realize, that THIS is it. THIS is who I am. Nothing stands between me and me. This bright, clear, intelligent awareness that is, indeed, transparent to the senses and thus overlooked is infinitely powerful and is who I am. For a little while I treated it as a subject of study—something to be investigated, something that needed coaxing to hang around. Now it reveals itself to be bright and perpetually present. How could it be otherwise?

The flatness and poignancy I was talking about have dispelled. What I have noticed is a deep and abiding engagement with what is. For decades, I have been following a story, my own personal soap opera, and the content of the story has had my attention. Now something deeper is being observed or realized. It is hard to describe but it is as though the content has a deep lovely liveliness to it. It, too, is alive. Everything that happens is precious. This is ironic, because in a sense I also know that what is happening has no meaning and is essentially unreal. I see the 'I' character as another piece of the mosaic, but its very transience somehow points to something deeply amazing that I had overlooked.

I do not want to wrap too many words around this. It is subtle and, as with all of this 'stuff', it shifts and changes. But I find myself wanting to use old-fashioned terms that are perhaps not politically correct in non-duality teachings. For example, I feel a great groundswell of heart-felt acceptance of everything in this story that has unfolded—all the characters, all the amazing, terrible and wonderful things that have transpired. It is like being awestruck by a sun set. At that moment you do not care how it works. You are just wordlessly amazed.

For someone as word-absorbed as myself, it is quite nice to reach the end of words and instead be simply stopped in one's tracks by what is. The story always had a purpose for me. I was always getting somewhere with it, dealing with it, waiting for it to deliver some goods I required. Now I am just sitting back in my seat and saying 'Wow!'

I wanted to share with you a poem by Cavafy, one of my favorite poets. The poem has been stuck on my kitchen cupboard for years. Maybe it will resonate with you. With heartfelt thanks for everything, John. I do not know how you have 'done' it, but everything is silently revealing itself. The urgency is over. I will continue to keep in touch. I enjoy sharing this. Thanks again for your wonderful books and your generosity. They are greatly appreciated.

Ithaca

As you set out for Ithaca
Hope your journey is a long one,
Full of adventure, full of discovery.

Keep Ithaca always in your mind.
Arriving there is what you are destined for.
But do not hurry the journey at all.
Better if it lasts for years,
So you are old by the time you reach the island,
Wealthy with all you've gained along the way,
Not expecting Ithaca to make you rich.

Ithaca gave you the marvelous journey.
Without her you would not have set out.
She has nothing left to give you now.
And if you find her poor, Ithaca will not have fooled you.
Wise as you have become, so full of experience,
You will have understood by then what these Ithacas mean.

John: Thank you for sharing your comments and experiences and the poem. Wonderful! It is amazing to find how all of this just simply reveals itself naturally and spontaneously. It is your sincere interest and deep love of life that has brought you back to the essence. How simple it is. I am glad you shared about how there is a natural embrace of life arising. Sometimes the appreciation of the non-dual pointers comes in at a mental level and the sheer grace and joy of living with this understanding is overlooked. That you can see and sense this is very good. As your experience shows, this is not dry philosophy at all, but an organic and natural flowering of something vital and full of life. There is really nothing that I can add, as you have expressed yourself quite beautifully indeed! You have a wonderful gift of expression. You may find, as I have, that there is a natural desire to share the beauty of this. Your writing here is a wonderful example.

89

In Awareness, There Is No Separation or Suffering

Questioner: I found your website a couple of months ago and started reading your articles. Almost immediately I began making sense of some of the things I had been reading by other authors and teachers. It was like sudden clear spots in a foggy landscape. One moment I could see. The next moment it might not be so clear. But not to worry. I am believing that seeing-knowing is still there, like the sun behind a cloud. Everything is here whether or not I am aware or not.

John: This is an important insight. Once it dawns on you that what you are looking for (the principle of being-awareness, which is your essential nature) is available and that it is there regardless of the appearances, you will naturally return to this recognition as a matter of course. The reminders can help for a period of time, so use them if they are helpful. At some point, the reminders are not needed because you have looked for yourself and seen what needs to be seen.

Q: Your book has been a big help. It has also contributed to an understanding that what I had imagined to be awakening probably has no relationship to what it really is.

John: Welcome to the club! This hung me up for a long time. I was seeking something, some great awakening or enlightenment that I felt I needed to achieve to 'get there'. In the end, this is discovered to be fallacious. What is most unexpected is that there is no awakening or enlightenment needed at all. The fact of awareness is already present and clear. It is just a recognition of something so simple and obvious that we overlooked it.

Q: I had imagined a state without anxiety, fear and so on, but I am beginning to wonder if that is really true.

John: Those self-centered states are generated by the belief in separation from the source. Once the basic position is clarified, those states naturally resolve because the root cause is taken care of. It is not really an attainment or yardstick to measure if 'you are there', but it is a natural corollary of clarifying your identity.

Q: This has all contributed to an 'I do not know anything' type of confusion akin to all of a sudden finding myself lost and disconnected from presence-awareness. I realize that I have not asked a question, and I am not sure what that would be, other than to say that this is where I am now. I am glad to have found you and your book.

John: Confusion is a mind state. It is an arising in thought that is generated by doubt and uncertainty. However, the fact of presence-awareness remains clear and constant and is not a matter of doubt. Just come back to the recognition that the mind's attempts to nail this down are all bound to fail. Certitude, clarity and peace arise from the direct, non-conceptual recognition of your real nature of presence-awareness. Once conceptual thought arises and you begin to follow it, you look away from the simplicity and clarity of presence-awareness and your identity as that. That is certain and beyond doubt.

People who say that doubt, fear, anxiety, questions and so on arising from the belief in a separate self continue, even with the recognition of who we are, are, in my view, not yet looking deeply enough and are advocating a partial understanding. They may not have looked deeply into the workings of suffering and realized that it is based on a series of underlying causes that can be resolved through clear seeing and understanding.

It is good to come back to the basic point that presence-awareness remains in spite of all thoughts and mind states. It is the unchanging and undeniable fact of being, which is ever-present and brightly aware. Without this, nothing else can appear. All appearances and states arise within awareness, but awareness is always free and untouched. It (you) is inherently free of confusion, doubt and suffering, just as the sun remains untouched and unsullied by whatever passes beneath it. You do not get to a state free of suffering. You discover that from the perspective of presence-awareness, which is what you truly are, there is no separation or suffering at all. Seeing this has the effect of unwinding all the false ideas and beliefs that generated suffering, starting with the core belief of being a limited and separate self. With that core belief dismantled through clear seeing, there is no basis for any subsequent self-centered thoughts and beliefs, and they all come undone through lack of any interest and attention. What remains is a steady sense of clarity and peace that does not leave you because it is inherent in the presence-awareness that you are.

Why Am I Awareness?

Questioner: You sometimes mention a sense of beingness or presence.

John: Yes.

Q: What sense of presence?

John: The sense of being, the sense of knowing that you are. If I ask, 'Do you exist?' you spontaneously answer 'Yes'. This is because you are undoubtedly present and aware.

Q: I thought any sense of something would be an appearance. I do not notice any sense of presence.

John: Because your being is not an object. It does not stand out in front of you as something apart. So you cannot sense it or know it with the senses or mind. Nonetheless, you cannot deny your existence or being at any time.

Q: I still cannot answer the question 'Are you aware?' because the word 'you' seems vague. How accurate with your words are you trying to be with that question?

John: Ultimately words fail because they are only symbols or pointers. They are not the things in themselves. So you need to look beyond the word to where it is pointing.

Q: I am sure a child would indeed answer that question quickly (lucky thing!), but a child would also say that the sky is blue. I can answer that 'there is awareness'. Is that good enough? And where would I go from there?

John: That is a good start. There is awareness. That is clear an undeniable. Awareness is the necessary support for any and all possible experiences. Without awareness, what can be there?

Q: Awareness is definitely here, but why am I that awareness? There is direct proof that I am not the body, mind and so on. But for the positive recognition, how do I know I am that? I do not want to just have the belief that I am awareness. What matters is the direct knowledge of it, right?

John: The mind is, in the end, completely useless for the non-conceptual recognition of awareness and your identity as that. You are realizing that the mind is fine for dealing with objects and appearances, but for dealing with awareness, it is not a sufficient tool. Simply put, awareness is not an object. It cannot be grasped, known or understood by the mind. That is why looking for proofs at the mind level about awareness and your identity as that are destined to fail.

You are stating something clear and correct when you say that awareness is definitely here. This is an undeniable and irrefutable fact of experience. You are also clear in saying that you are not the body and mind. At this point, it appears that you are concerned with being certain that this presence of awareness is, in fact, what you are. Here are a few pointers to consider in this regard.

You never, under any circumstances, observe awareness as an object apart from you. Body, senses and mind appear as objects known. They arise and set and can be clearly observed as passing appearances before us. But you cannot say this of awareness. Because you and awareness are never observed apart from each other, you and awareness must be the same thing. That is, what you are and what awareness is are synonymous. The words are two, but what they point to is one.

You have seen that you are nothing objective (body, senses or mind). Awareness, also, is nothing objective. Something that is non-objective has no characteristics by which it could be distinguished from another non-objective thing. In fact, how could there even be two non-objective things, as there is nothing by which they could be differentiated? This also points to the fact that your nature and awareness are one and the same thing.

Everyone instinctively says, 'I exist. I am aware'. This is a self-evident fact that needs no proof or verification. You say that you are certain that there is awareness but unclear as to the identity of the 'I' as that. This is a clear intuition because it exposes the fact that the seeming separate 'I' does not really exist, except as a notion or idea appearing in the awareness. You are coming upon the key insight that there is no separate self existing independently from awareness. The seeming arising of some separate 'I' or self apart from awareness has never happened. All there is, is awareness. There is no separate individual who stands apart from that.

So the assumed separate 'I' is not, and awareness is present beyond any doubt. Still, all people have the undeniable and irrefutable sense of being present and aware. This can only mean that they do not exist as separate individuals, but as the principle of pure awareness itself, which shines beyond all thought and concepts, including 'I', 'you' and any other that the mind can generate.

To sum up, the principle of awareness is an undeniable fact. You do not exist as any kind of separate self apart from that because you cannot observe that any such separation has occurred. The seeming separate 'I' is a fiction, because it is never observed. The individual 'I' is absent. When looked for, all that is found is awareness. However, that awareness is not a metaphysical principle shining 'out there' as some intangible presence. It shines in the core of each living being as its fundamental identity. That is why various pointers are used, such as 'the Self', 'your real nature' and so on. The great non-dualistic traditions say that 'All there is, is being-awareness, and you are that'. This points to the fundamental unity of our essential self and the principle of being-awareness that is the substratum of the apparent cosmos.

At a practical level, this boils down to the recognition that the principle of awareness is what is finally real. We come to recognize that this is available and present within us and is ultimately what we truly are. This awareness is timeless, unchanging, free and peaceful by nature. The non-conceptual knowing of the principle of awareness and our identity as that uproots all belief in separation and undercuts all the self-centered suffering and doubts predicated on that belief. It is the realization of non-duality or oneness. All seeking, doubts and suffering are conclusively resolved.

91

I Am What I Seek

Questioner: It is good to share what is. I find that 'it' somehow enlivens when it is spoken about or written about. It is funny, but I recall feeling this sense of wholeness and certainty as a baby and toddler! Everything simply was, and there was nothing to do about it—just enjoy. Although of course there were no words.

I recall going to school (I had very religious parents) and realizing that there were conditions that had to be met. Suddenly the world of theory was upon me, although of course I had no idea that that was what it was. I was so innocent. Why should I disbelieve anything that was being told to me by those who clearly loved me?

But I moved from being self-sufficient and whole—from being enough and joyous—into a world in which I could never quite measure up. I am an artistic soul and have always lived in a creative imagination, and this was derided and belittled. The only constant thing I can remember from school, which I hated, was constantly being told to come back from my dream world. Eventually, of course, obedience took hold. I thought there was something wrong with me and right with 'them'. I struggled and strived for intellectual competency, which was ironic really, because I became acutely miserable and spent the subsequent three decades being berated by spiritual teachers for being too intellectual!

In short, from my distorted perception, there has always been something wrong with me that others have been able to put right. I now see my years in spiritual search as a sort of continuation of what happened at school, but in reverse. There is always some guru or teacher at the front who has the answers, who knows better, who can put me right. I am always in some posture of reverence or deference, never quite finding what I already have. It has been ridiculous.

I think this is probably the experience of 'apparent others' too. We have had it drummed into us that theorizing is central to things, and it is very difficult to backtrack, to actually trust that innocent 'tabula rasa' which we were told to relinquish when we were three years old. And it seems that this is where all the questions arise from—that relentless need to intellectually enquire that is so much a part of the western mind set.

What has happened for me is twofold. I have realized that inquiry leads nowhere. Or rather, answers can be provided, but they are provisional because they are only pointers. They are not what actually is. Gradually it has dawned on me that I was reading and rereading a menu rather than sitting down to eat! And, in addition to this, there is the emergent realization of what is already known. It is as though wafting smells from the kitchen are impinging on conscious awareness and the menu loses its charm!

It was quite a shock a few days ago to stop in my tracks and realize that this—this experience, this simple being—is it, that I am what I seek. In fact, there was almost a sense of resignation, the certainty that this is it so I better get used to it! And as I settle in with that certainty, and the force of the searching begins to die away, there is seen to be great power and strength in that simple being, the simple being towards which these words are simply pointing.

I used to pick up your book for sustenance. These days, I will read a bit and then need to set the book aside, because what has been pointed to is so vibrantly alive that it is a more engaging experience than reading about it. Experience of course is not quite the right word, but you know what I mean.

The other thing that is observed is the sheer familiarity of 'it'. When it is observed that something is familiar, questions fall away. It is like meeting a stranger and asking lots of questions then realizing you are talking to your own child. The questions become utterly redundant.

I also love the fact that it is all so much simpler than I was led to believe. All those complex spiritual traditions I belonged to! All the things one had to do in order to be worthy! Always wearing black, or never wearing black. Only eating pure food, or always eating what you want. Expressing the truth exactly how you feel, or only saying things that are uplifting. So many complications and contradictions—and how the mind loved it! I see how these traditions feed on confusion rather than clarity, all that worthiness and waiting, when all that is being pointed to is this simple unadorned awareness and the riches that abide silently therein when one stops to look.

Thank you for encouraging me to write about this. I feel things are settling in, and when they are settled then, yes, that is what I shall probably do, if only for the selfish reason that I have observed that what you put your attention on gets stronger in your life. So many false starts have been fed with my attention. For now, the awareness moves to the awareness. Awareness is aware of itself. I want to let that rest for a while, and yes, if I may, to keep in touch.

I cannot describe how grateful I have been for your clarity. So many teachers avoid the thorny questions or berate the student for asking them. But you do not duck the ball. You catch it and run with it. After all, I know that the mind cannot access the truth, any more than the eyes can look on the back of the head, but if words charmed us away from the simplicity of what is, then they can point back to it. I feel I have no questions any more, but I would like to share what I feel, what continues to emerge.

John: You express yourself beautifully. I have enjoyed your sharing of all this. It is clear that the simplicity of this has struck home. It is not an intellectual appreciation but a lived and felt experience. Your words show this. Because you write and express yourself so well, I am sure you will find ways to use that ability not only to confirm your own experience and understanding, but also in ways that will impact others who might be looking for some pointers, just as you once were. The greatest way to return the favor is just to pass it along to others who may be interested. Passing along the message is like pouring wine from a bottomless container. The more you give it away, the more there is to give. You are on your way with this. I look forward to seeing what unfolds from this point. Feel free to stay in touch and let me know how things are going.

92

Words Are Not of the Essence

Questioner: I have just finished your book *Awakening to the Natural State*, which I very much enjoyed. I look forward to reading 'Shining in Plain View'. My question, if I may ask, regards the nature of presence-awareness. This appears to equate with Sri Nisargadatta's 'I am', beingness or consciousness.

John: Nisargadatta has his own usage of terms, which is sometimes different from what others use. This is due to his own language, that of his teacher and also translation issues. So it is easy to go astray in trying to understand the words. This is just another confirmation that the words are not of the essence.

Nisargadatta nearly always uses the terms 'being' and 'consciousness' as appearances within the dualistic manifestation. Thus he says that what you are is 'prior to consciousness, prior to beingness'. In his terms, 'beingness' and 'consciousness' are arisings that depend on the psychosomatic apparatus. Let us not even get into gunas, prana and the rest of it! In 'I Am That' he states that you are that pure awareness that witnesses the rising and falling of consciousness. Obviously, the terminology is different than what is used, for example, by other well-known teachers, such as Ramana Maharshi or Shankara, who use 'consciousness' as synonymous with the unchanging reality or absolute.

You must realize that you are dealing with terminology issues. That is one reason why meeting 'Sailor' Bob Adamson was very helpful to me. Trying to figure this all out at a mental level is pretty much hopeless. It is much easier than all that!

I tend to favor a simpler wording. So in my terms, the sense of knowing, awareness or being in you to which the mind and all else appears, is the same as what Nisargadatta calls the 'pure awareness' that watches the rise and fall of what he refers to as 'consciousness'.

Q: In what I have read, Nisargadatta appears to distinguish between consciousness and the Absolute (Parabrahman), which is beyond the 'I am'.

John: That pure, non-objective awareness in you which knows the thought-feeling 'I am' and all else is what is pointed to as the reality. The Nisargadatta books use terms derived from medieval Hindu metaphysics. Unless you get into all that and really nail down the translations and understand the context, the wording can be confusing (at least it was for me). Fortunately, that is not necessary.

As Bob Adamson once told me when I was asking him similar questions to yours about Nisargadatta's language: 'Notice that when you try to figure out what someone else meant, you move away from the simple and direct knowing of your own nature, that undeniable sense of presence-awareness that you cannot leave'. In other words, trying to understand Nisargadatta's words is not really necessary in the end and, in fact, can be a roadblock. Each teacher may use different words and terms and will adapt and modify the language as needed.

Q: You state all spiritual seeking ended when your 'I' was seen as non-existent, and it was realized that there is only presence-awareness. But, in fact, is not there still the Absolute to be realized (albeit by no one)?

John: No. In my wording, the presence-awareness is the same as the absolute. It is the ultimate backstop. Everything that can possibly appear is just a movement in the presence-awareness that you are. Any apparent realization would just be a transient experience in that. The notion of a realization beyond this is just an idea in the awareness that you are.

With the absence of any individual, no realizations are needed, for as you have intuited, there is no one present to have them. All the realizations and attainments are for the imagined individual. With that out of the picture, everything falls to pieces and the seeking is done. As they say, 'All there is, is non-conceptual, self-shining, ever-fresh, presence-awareness, just this and nothing else'.

Q: I am grateful for your taking the time to clear this up for me.

John: See how that does. This all came to me during discussions I had with Bob Adamson, who had been with Nisargadatta for many months probing into all this with him. So it comes down by direct contact, which is an invaluable and necessary supplement to what is recorded in the books. Anyway, you are present and aware. That is it. The simplicity of it is generally overlooked.

Follow up ...

Q: You have been most helpful and clear. I believe understanding is essential in all this, and in the last year I have managed to rid myself of a lot of doubts and gain some intellectual understanding. Without such a basis I doubt I would be in the position to go beyond the intellect with any sustained conviction. I now feel ready and able to do that, whatever the mind may throw up.

John: I am glad to hear that the basics are becoming clear now. It is important to see that the mind or intellect is useful only as a pointer and that the essence that you are is not a matter of mental understanding. You will see as you continue to probe into this that the present awareness that you are is, by nature, already free of the mind. That awareness is what thoughts, feelings and perceptions arise within, yet it is not caught or limited by that which appears. It is always present and shining upstream of the mind. So, you do not bring in something new or attain any realization that was not already present. You discover the truth of what your being actually is. All that hung us up was that we were under a mistaken impression and were looking for the answer elsewhere. When this gets pointed out, you stop and have a look. Then you see that what the books have been pointing to and that what you have been seeking is what you already are. The simplicity of it is the key. The fact of being, which is present as that sense of awareness or knowing in you, is what is to be recognized. Not seeing this, we took ourselves to be something we were not—hence, all the trouble. A bit of investigation and clear seeing will clarify things straight away.

Your True Nature Is Inescapable

Question: The painful fog is gone. Everything seems very clear—joyful, actually. The conceptual tricks telling me that 'peace will be gone as soon as the teacher goes home' are not pulling me in. I am amazed at how subtle and frequent those 'I am not there yet' concepts were. Dozens of them have been stopped in their tracks and questioned since you left.

Several things are very clear. I do not think I will fall for the notion of coming and going out of awareness again. That is not to say the concepts do not keep arising to try to cloud the truth, but consistently it is seen that awareness never leaves. And that what I am is not separate from awareness.

I have been relentlessly looking for 'Jane', and I found her! She is in all the stories appearing in awareness. She is very social, very talkative with many other characters and prods this body to take action based on conversations that never took place! I found time, too. It is in every story, but strangely, it disappears when I come back to present awareness. And darned if I can find 'Jane' anywhere else. I am not giving up the search yet because I am not sure she will be back and up to her old tricks. I am looking for her around every possible corner until I know with certainty that she will not be back stirring the conceptual pot.

I have also been looking for the 'others'. I have only found them in two places. They are either talking with 'me' in my self-centered thought conversations, or they are objects arising in my awareness. I cannot find a separate 'me' and cannot find a separate 'other'.

I am sure I will have more questions. Right now I am on

a quest to uncover the truth, or remove the conceptual veil, once and for all.

John: All sounds good. Keep up the looking and let the simplicity of presence-awareness burn through any residual doubts and concepts. There is no need to wait any longer. Time is a concept. All there is, is now, and in that now, your true nature is clear, present and inescapable. Stand as that and nothing can touch you.

Follow up ...

Q: Thank you for continuing to dialogue with me for a while. After spending much time on looking at the conceptual 'I' from all viewpoints I am pretty well done with it. I am very much down to just watching the conceptual me-clouds continue to rise up to be questioned. Then I question them and they are quickly gone, taking me back to awareness. For the most part, that is an extremely positive experience—peaceful, warm and fuzzy. One night I experienced real joy that came in waves. Then there are periods looking at this bright, shining awareness that are not so bright and shiny. In fact, it is pretty dull and lifeless. I try to see it as just a dull and lifeless conceptual fog that has to be looked at the same way as more obvious self-centered me thoughts. It is working pretty well.

John: Remember that experiences, such as dull or lifeless feelings, are states arising in the appearance, in the content of awareness. Awareness is never dull or lifeless. It is life itself. It continuously shines on all that appears, infusing each and every experience with presence and knowing. If clouds or fog appeared in the sky, it would be wrong to say that the sun became dull or without light. The sun always remains as it is. It is the same with presence or awareness. It always remains as it is. The habit has been to look away from this and focus on the appearance. Then we gauge the level of aliveness or clarity through the states of body and mind that are arising in the moment. A slight shift of focus back to what is present and aware in you is all that is needed to recognize that all that has happened is that a bit of focus has gone into thought. The clarity of your real essence did not vanish, but was only overlooked.

Q: It is certainly a collage of experiences, but I am very focused on the basics. If you ask me if there is still a 'me', the only way I know to answer that for now is to say that there are still 'me' thoughts that arise to be questioned. And questioned they are.

John: This is a key insight and very important to explore. When you look into the 'me', you find that there are thoughts, concepts, beliefs and ideas about the 'me'. This leads to the presumption that the 'me' is present. We think that it must be real and substantial. But the question is, apart from all the thoughts and ideas, is there actually something present that is the 'me'? It is the belief in the presence of a substantial existing 'me' that is the root and origin of separation and all the attendant suffering that follows this belief. All suffering appears in the form of self-centered thinking that sprouts from the assumption that the 'I' or 'me' is real and that this is what we are.

The end of suffering dawns when this belief is investigated and exposed as false. All of the suffering, doubts, questions, seeking and so on, are always for that separate 'me' which imagines itself as defective and incomplete. We take ourselves to be that limited self and take all the self-centered concepts to be true. This belief in the self-center and the subsequent embrace of the self-centered ideas as true is what suffering is—nothing more, nothing less. The direct inquiry into the reality of the central I-thought pulls the plug on the entire network of self-centered beliefs. To discover that there is, in fact, no 'me' present at all completely undercuts the whole network of self-centered beliefs at a single stroke.

This is why simply watching thoughts, as a spiritual exercise, is ineffective as a means to freedom from suffering. The core mechanism at work is not brought to light and exposed. The assumption of being a separate, limited 'me' goes on in full swing. After all, who is doing the watching and why? Only a presumed separate 'me' would feel compelled to pick up an exercise to get free. Without seeing this, the exercise only heightens the belief in the self center.

Q: There is still a tendency to want to sort of hole up and protect this, as if I can handle the thoughts arising in a quiet house, while being less sure of a real 'test' in the relational world. This implies there are still doubts to be looked at. They are just more subtle in how they present themselves, I guess. At any rate, I am very clear on the basics.

John: Keep in mind that the presence-awareness that you are is always clear and present, regardless of circumstances. There cannot be any circumstances without your existence and awareness there to register them. You can recognize your true nature anywhere and any place. No events, experiences, thoughts, feelings or states can be an obstacle. They are all arising in the awareness that you are. They are all just pointers back the ever-present and undeniable awareness that you can never leave.

Do not focus the doubts and questions. These are just remnant habits and thoughts being generated in the mind, which is overlooking that the answer is already present and clear. Your being, your presence, your awareness, whatever name we call it, is utterly present and beyond doubt. The mind cannot offer any resistance to this recognition. To give attention to the doubts and question is a residual habit of looking for the answer in the mind.

Just see that all the doubts and suffering are self-centered thoughts appearing in the mind. They are based on a presumption of being something limited and apart. When you investigate this, you do not find any separate 'me' present at all. What you find yourself to be is the undeniable fact of being-awareness. Take up your headquarters there. Then you will look upon the world of appearance as from a lofty peak. From the position of presence-awareness, which is where you always reside, no doubts, questions, problems or suffering can touch you, just as clouds can never touch the sun.

There Is Something To Do—Understand

Questioner: While your postings invariably produce peace, I seem to be waiting for permanent change—the event of awakening, no matter what you say about it not being needed.

John: It is good to be precisely clear on things. My postings do not produce peace! At most, they point to the presence of the true nature in you, which is the one and only source of lasting peace there is. We continue to wait for awakenings, realizations and other experiences because we believe that peace is not present and that some event will happen to deliver it. But this is an exercise in futility. To clearly recognize and understand our true nature is all that is required to discover lasting peace. Your true nature is that simple presence of being and awareness that is with you right now. Not grasping the simplicity of this, we wait for awakenings and look away from the source of peace within. The belief in the need for awakening is a subtle concept that is attractive only until the simplicity of what is being pointed out is appreciated. You need no awakening because your essential nature is already present with you and is already clarity and awareness itself. It just comes down to stopping and recognizing this now.

Q: Just now it struck me that effort is the problem because effort can only be mind and not awareness. OK, that means I should stop trying. But then, trying not to try seems hopeless.

John: Effort can only be in the mind. Effort implies getting something that is not present. But how much effort do you need to be present and aware? Is this not going on effortlessly all the time? Although no effort is needed, there can be an understanding of what is pointed to. It is wrong to say there is nothing to do. There is most certainly something to do, and that is to understand what is being pointed to. It is all about understanding, not doing something in particular. We suffer and have doubts because we are under a misapprehension about who and what we are. To resolve the doubts and suffering it is incumbent upon us to investigate what is true about ourselves and resolve the issue of our identity. To see what is true about ourselves and question the false identity is most certainly necessary. Otherwise, the pointers remain merely intellectual knowledge.

Trying and not trying are from the position of an entity that believes it is separate and must do something to regain wholeness. Not trying is just another doing—trying to give up trying! As you can see, that line of approach ties one up in knots. The reason is that the basic position is still not yet seen. There is nothing to try or not try to do because what you are seeking is already present as your own conscious self. Presence-awareness is. It is not a matter of trying or not trying. It is just a matter of seeing what is clear and obvious in you right now. There is no harm in looking at the pointers in order to verifying them for yourself. In fact, this is very useful. It is also the most direct path to understanding your true nature and dispelling the false beliefs that drive our doubts and confusion.

Q: As for finding the absence of the 'I' or the presence of shining awareness, I am drawing a blank there. Please clarify.

John: Start with the fact of the presence of awareness. You are present. You are aware. This is doubtlessly true because you are here now, fully present and registering all the thoughts, feelings and perceptions arising. Is there any doubt about the fact of your own being? This is what is being pointed out as your true nature. There is nothing mysterious about it. It is fully present and shining in plain view at all times. Begin to explore this a bit and let the pointers resonate. We are very apt to overlook the simplicity of this.

The absence of the 'I' means that there is nothing that you can see, think of or perceive that is your real, essential self. All those things come and go, but you remain. We usually overlook the fact that what we are is the principle of being or awareness. Instead, we imagine ourselves to be something objective, something knowable by the senses or mind. But the awareness that you are is not knowable by the senses or mind, because those things are appearances in awareness itself. Awareness is upstream of the organs of sensing, feeling and knowing. Yet this presence that you are is not mysterious or unknowable. It is the light of awareness that is constantly illuminating everything that appears at all times and all places. It is the essence of what you are even now, even though it may been have overlooked. No living being can deny that they are present and aware. This very presence-awareness is pointed out as the reality that we have been seeking. Once this is seen, the game is up. You are that right now, so just stop and have a look at what is being pointed to. Without your awareness, nothing else can be.

95

There Is Nothing Greater Than This

Questioner: How lovely to hear from you! I was just in the process of printing out the contents of your website, as I am going away for a few days to camp with my son. I felt it would be a lovely opportunity to further immerse myself in all this (wrong words, but you know what I mean). It was funny to come across my words on your site—a very beautiful experience! Like a reflection of myself that I did not quite recognize.

It is funny how quickly it all appears to change. I was also listening this morning to the radio show on which you appeared, and I loved the reference to the clouds being unable to obscure the sun when seen from the perspective of the sun. That sun-and-clouds analogy is a well-worn image in spiritual circles, isn't it? And more and more I realize—as I settle in with all this—that far from wanting to say 'it has gone away!' as I would have said of consciousness a few weeks ago, that I am more likely to remark 'sometimes thoughts come'. There has been a subtle shift in weight, if you like, an almost tangible implosion (at least it feels like an implosion), an almost physical feeling of deeply letting go, as it is deeply realized that this is unfolding precisely as it should. The urgency I used to feel, the sense that there was something to get, some race against time I was losing, is gradually losing its power. This silent, still, bright, solid, transparent, never-changing thing that I am just playfully reveals itself.

The obviousness of it stops me in my tracks. This is hard to put into words, but it is the sheer reality of it that arrests me. I mean, this is it, isn't it? There is nothing behind it, nothing beyond it. This is what has been sought all along. And then obvious extensions of that deep-felt realization also arise. Like if this is all there is—and when you stop to look at it, that is obviously the case—then there is nothing else. So it is slowly dawning on me that there can be no fear, because there is only this. There is no God, no guru, no other. There is simply nothing greater than this And this is beyond greatness. When I look at it, I can attempt to describe its qualities (still, silent, intelligent, ever-fresh and so on), but I could not say what size it is. It is dimensionless.

Thank you again John for your generosity. I find it such a joy to share what I am experiencing. I feel fairly sure that I will share one day, for now I am just settling in with this, sharing with you and a couple of friends. After all the go-getting of a frenetic life's search, it is nice just to unwind with it, to savor its depths. And that is something else, the depths to this, the subtleties which are revealed when I pause to attend to it. I am discovering subtle senses I did not know I had, super-senses, if you like. I do not mean in the sense of superwoman or anything like that! Just immense subtlety. For the first time in my life, I feel able to just be with something and get to know it. After all, I was a long time searching.

Thank you again for your time, your guidance and your kindness. Words cannot express my appreciation.

John: Thank you for sending along your thoughtful and clearly expressed comments. The basics are right with you now and clearly in view. Everything unfolds spontaneously in the presence-awareness that you are. Without the belief in a separate self-center in the picture, the questions and doubts are drained of all their energy. You are left in the clarity and immediacy of undeniable being. It is the constant, benevolent background which supports and embraces any and all appearances and arisings. Knowing that you can never leave that, no matter what appears, everything is all right as it is. Thinking, acting, living, expressing—whatever it might be—all comes up as an uncalculated expression in each moment. My friend Bob Adamson has a wonderful phrase he uses, 'effortless living'. There is just a wonder and easy joy as each moment reveals itself within and upon that clear presence of awareness that never leaves you. Now you know.

Your writing is coming out very clearly and beautifully expressed. Keep your writings tucked away. You may find a means of sharing your expressions at some point, if the spirit moves. I am sure many people would be delighted to hear what you are sharing.

Awareness Is Not Thought—Or Is It?

Questioner: I have a question regarding a statement that appeared in one of your articles. It reads: 'As I say, thoughts, feelings and sensations arise in awareness. Ultimately, they are nothing but that awareness, because they have no independent existence apart from it'. Here is my question. I am not my thoughts. I know this because I am aware of them. Because I am aware of them, I cannot be them. Thoughts, feelings and sensations arise in awareness. They are not awareness. Your statement implies that I am my thoughts, feelings and sensations, because you say they (thoughts) have no independent existence apart from awareness. But this is impossible! There is some confusion here for me. Can you clarify?

John: It looks as if you are reading the material carefully and trying to get to the bottom of things! That is good.

To start off with, it is helpful to recap the basic and fundamental pointer that everything gets down to. You are present and aware. When you begin to probe into this, you find that you are not a being who has presence and awareness (or presence-awareness, for short), but you are presence-awareness itself. Objects come and go, but you remain as the ever-present awareness itself. To see this deeply is all the understanding that is required. Until we probe into this, we are apt to mistake our identity to be a limited person, identified with the body and mind. This mistaken identity is the source of confusion and suffering. Clarifying our real identity is the aim of the spiritual pointers. With our real nature clearly recognized, the root of the confusion is exposed and the questioning, seeking and suffering naturally fall away (because the root cause is removed). Our identity as presence-awareness is clear and beyond doubt.

Let me say a few words about spiritual pointers. All the pointers are just ways to bring us back to the core understanding of who and what we are. They are not necessarily consistent in all aspects because they often take up different angles of vision or different questions or are addressed to people with differing concerns.

One pointer is that you are not thought. This can be clearly seen, as you have noted, because thoughts come and go while you remain. Thoughts are objects, but you are the knower of them. This pointer is very useful when we are focused on thought and assume that our identity is wrapped up in thoughts. Many of us have not even considered the possibility that our deeper essence lies beyond thought. To see ourselves as the witness of thought or the unchanging awareness behind thought is a powerful insight that severs the exclusive identification with the mind. This pointer primarily applies when the thoughts are taken as real and substantial entities and there is a feeling of identification with them. Of course, these assumptions are incorrect, but the pointer is a means of countering these false assumptions. In the first pointer, we are looking into our own nature (awareness). To get this more clearly in view, we note that thoughts are not our essence. This allows the presence-awareness to be recognized more clearly.

There is another way of viewing thought that at first blush appears contradictory. This pointer says that thought is awareness itself. This comes in at a bit deeper level of understanding. Once we have seen our real nature as presence-awareness and this has come to the forefront, so to speak, we can look back at thought, not from the position of trying to be free from it or to clarify our identity, but rather to look into the nature of thought itself to understand its nature. When you begin to probe into thought to understand what it is, several interesting things come to light.

First of all, thought only ever exists when it is appearing in awareness. It cannot stand separate and apart. It has no real substance or independent nature at all. It is a vibration or movement in the awareness itself. As waves rise and set in the sea, so do thoughts arise and set in awareness itself. Waves are nothing but the sea. They may appear as entities separate from the sea, but in fact are they not. In the same way, thoughts, perceptions and feelings arise and set in awareness. If they arise from awareness, have no real existence apart from awareness, and merge into awareness, then their ultimate substance must be awareness itself. This is where non-duality comes in. All there is, is awareness. Ultimately, there is nothing else. Everything is just an appearance on or within awareness. In essence, everything is that awareness, just like all the waves in the sea are nothing but the sea.

This second pointer is an extension to the first one and completes it. The first pointer is useful to clarify your identity and end the false beliefs and suffering based on believing yourself to be something you are not. The second pointer follows on by absorbing all the seeming appearances back into your essence and showing how nothing stands apart from this. This undercuts any remaining sense of duality or separation and establishes the final position that all there is, is non-duality or oneness.

Both pointers are only that—pointers. The fact is what you are. That remains as the undeniable presence of awareness that you can never leave. Nothing with any substantial or independent nature has ever existed apart from this. It is not necessary to understand or apply all the various pointers. However, if you do investigate them a bit, you will see that they all converge back to the core revelation that what you are seeking is what you already are—that ever-free, ever-complete and perfect principle of being-awareness that is completely clear and beyond doubt at all times. This is your nature, and it is also the nature of everything else that seems to appear. It is all one nature or one substance: awareness itself. This is what you are.

97

All Doubts and Questions Arise in Present Awareness

Questioner: Your dialogues are great. They are 'spot on', as our UK friends say. I enjoyed your response to my statement that I was not sure if the 'me' is there but there are still 'me thoughts' that arise to be questioned. Of course! The 'me' that arises in thought is the only 'me' in town! I was still looking for another 'me' somewhere!

John: Excellent. Let me know when and if you find such a thing!

Q: I know we have been through all this before (a few times) but this time is different. It was what you said about simply seeing all the doubts and questions as self-centered thought arising in present awareness. It has not been the same since. After a 'little bit of looking', as you like to say, I just do not give credence to what comes up in thought.

John: This is the key. To finally realize that what thought has been telling us about ourselves is not true brings down the curtain on the life of suffering and seeking.

Q: The compulsive thinking seems to have stopped. Thinking arises. Self-centered thinking arises but is significantly less and is caught practically as soon it appears. It is looked at or questioned and moves right through and back to present awareness. There is definitely a lightness, an ease and an engagement with life.

John: This is excellent and shows you are seeing clearly and the pointers are striking home.

Q: I realized too something that was really a conceptual roadblock for me, and that is that I have been dismissing a lot of these pointers with 'Oh, I know that'. Suffering arises from the idea of a separate 'me'? 'Oh, I know that'. So who is the arrogant one that knows all that? And am I ready to look at this fresh from—hello-o-o!— my direct experience?

John: Yes. We may have heard all this, sometimes for years! But eventually it comes down to having a look for ourselves to verify things in our own direct experience. This happens when it dawns on us that understanding who we are and freedom from doubt are truly possible. Then the motivation is there to seriously consider what is being pointed out.

Q: There is definitely a shift in focus. It is much more in present awareness than in thought.

John: Very good. To establish your center of gravity, so to speak, in the presence-awareness that you are is what it comes down to. Of course, we always were that all along. But if we had known it, we would not have the suffering and doubts in the first place. To have an initial recognition of our identity as awareness is a starting point, but much more fruitful is the deep and abiding recognition of this. This undercuts the tendency to return to seeking our identity in thought.

Q: It feels as if I have climbed to the top of the mountain and am coming down the other side. I just cannot see getting lost in self-centered suffering again at this point. Something has broken open. I can see where it comes from now so I cannot imagine being tricked again.

John: Yes. Once you see what is going on in full clarity, you cannot be fooled again. Even if a habit or false belief comes in, you cannot stick with it for long because you have seen what is true.

Q: When I started into (yet again) another round of suffering before your talk, there was an understanding that I did not have to do this anymore.

John: You have recognized that suffering is no longer necessary. You have seen the underlying mechanism and now understand what is happening. From that position, there is less and less interest or ability to feed into the self-centered thoughts any longer.

Q: I have always said that everything I needed was in your dialogues. So it was time to get to the root of the suffering. The desire to end suffering is finally greater than its attraction, I guess. Thank you for your persistence and staying the course with me. I am very grateful.

John: It is wonderful to see this settling in for you in your direct experience. That is what it is all about. Eventually, you come back to the essence of things and have a look to see what is really going on. A desire arises to get to the root of things and clarify your real identity. A life of suffering, confusion and doubt is no longer satisfactory. Once you understand that the origin of suffering lies in the mistaken belief in who you are, you lose interest in the personality and its network of self-centered thoughts and stories. Then you see it for what it is—just a series of unexamined ideas and beliefs with no real basis at all. With the focus off the ideas and stories in thought, you easily and directly reclaim your natural identity of simple presence-awareness. It is marvelous to finally discover how clear and obvious this is. It can be seen and understood in an instant, because it is always shining right here in plain view. That is the long and short of it.

You Have Everything You Need

Questioner: The last two days everything has been happening on its own. I have no desire to keep reading all the dialogues now, so I am just being with this. The thoughts are really flowing through with little attention, and I notice very few self-centered thoughts. The mind feels clear, and that is a big relief. There is no self-centered involvement that I can see. There were a number of circumstances that I would be in before that would just automatically bring up a slew of self-centered thoughts. I have been in a number of those circumstances now, and it was wonderful to just enjoy the circumstance without all of the negative 'me stuff' arising.

John: Good news.

Q: It seems remarkable, and yet it is very ordinary. Even the sweetness that comes seems quite ordinary, although I do recognize that it is coming from a deep well-spring within me rather than caused by some external circumstance. If this were happening on its own without previous information, I would not associate it with anything spiritual.

John: Even now, there is no need to associate this as being something spiritual. Awareness, your real essence, is neither spiritual nor worldly. It is as it is. It is the fact of presence-awareness. Everything that can be said is just a label or comment by the mind. At some point, you move beyond the need for labels and words. There is just the direct, wordless, non-conceptual recognition of your own being.

Q: The sense of 'no me' comes from inferring from what is happening for the most part, rather than some other-worldly experience of it. There is a clear sense of life arising on its own without my involvement.

John: The sense of 'no me' is not an inference or otherworldly experience. It is a direct recognition based on looking, here and now, that there is no separate entity in the picture at all. As you are discovering in your direct experience, there is simply life arising without the need for involvement with an imaginary sense of self.

Q: I had another experience of waves of love, but it came and went, so I did not attach anything to that except pure enjoyment.

John: Let any experience come. As it comes, so it will go. But you ever remain as you are. What you are is pure being, pure awareness and pure love itself. What comes and goes is not real love, but the expression or reflection of love in the appearance. Just as you cannot grasp hold of the reflection of your face in a mirror, so you cannot find love 'out there' as an experience. The light of awareness is love, because it is the all-embracing ground that enfolds all of existence and makes it possible.

Q: There is a strong sense of being with what is right in front of me most of the time. I cannot find it now, but somewhere in your writings you talked about this becoming clearer and clearer as it unfolds. Yes?

John: You are ready to get beyond the 'things becoming clearer and clearer' phase. Present awareness is what you are here and now. Any doubt about that? Discard any subtle tendency of the mind to push understanding into the future. At this point, go to the essence. If not now, when? See that you do not need that thought. You do not need to wait around any longer for some unfolding. That is said at a certain stage for encouragement so that you will be willing to have a look and stick with the seeing of what is present. For you now, this is clearly recognized. The pointers have done their work and you do not need them. Simply stand as this undeniable and inescapable presence-awareness that you are. Abide with the firm conviction that you are that.

Look straight through any thought or belief that says you are bound, separate or incomplete in any way whatsoever. Present awareness is the reality. It is here and now in all its fullness. You are not separate from that. The past and future do not exist, except as imaginings that can arise only now. There is no understanding to attain because everything that you were ever hoping to find is shining right at your center. There is no search and nothing to get. Those concepts are false because they lead you away from the simple recognition of what is clear and present. Any number of insights and revelations can and will arise, but they will be flowerings right in the presence-awareness that you are and which cannot leave. No realizations, unfoldings or awakenings are needed. Those, too, are concepts to be discarded.

You now have everything you could possibly need. In the end, there is only one thing you really need—and that is the fact of your own being. The good news is that it is always with you. It is the one thing that you can never lose.

Q: I can see how the tricky, subtle mind stuff tries to come back in and complicate things! OK, I will stand firm in the conviction that it is done and come back to what I am.

John: Remember, present awareness IS. All attainments and subtle movements toward it are conceptual illusions. It is not a realization, just a seeing of what is shining in plain view.

Discard every notion to the contrary. This leaves you as what you are. And what else can you be but what you already are? All that ever happens is that appearances arise, swirl around a bit and then naturally depart, leaving you as you are—ever present, ever aware and ever clear. It is just like the sun shining down on the mountains and the desert. It effortlessly illumines everything, yet remains untouched and free from whatever is going on below. You are the sun of pure awareness. The world in all of its myriad forms and appearances unfolds in your light.

99

You Are Nothing—and Everything

Questioner: I would like to follow up on our previous discussion contained in the article 'Awareness Is Not Thought—Or Is It?' You likened thoughts in awareness to waves rising in the sea. I think part of the problem is the oneness you refer to. Is it that the waves merge back into the sea but the sea cannot merge with the waves? In other words, are the waves the content of the sea, but not vice versa? In like manner, can we view thoughts (mind) as the content of awareness? But awareness cannot be the content of the thoughts, can it? I am not so sure of this either. The mind might be doing the talking right now!

John: There is not much need to sort through all this. It tends to activate the mind and keep us on the boil looking for some understanding that we imagine we do not have. You said your nature as awareness is clear. Stabilize on that point. Awareness is the reality. Now you know this is what you are. This recognition alone is enough to end the belief in being a limited, separate self and usher in immense peace and clarity.

The other pointer (of thought being nothing but awareness) is a tailpiece to conclude things. If the question arises concerning the nature of the appearances (including thoughts, feelings and perceptions), you can see that everything that arises appears right in awareness itself. We never experience anything as a separate, independent or substantial thing apart from awareness. Because those things never stand apart from awareness, they must be, in the final analysis, awareness. Awareness is the substance or content of which they are made.

Let us go back to the wave analogy. Is any given wave the actual sea? No. It is a movement or appearance on the sea. But can the wave stand apart from the sea? No. It has no independent nature as a thing apart. So, is any given thought the actual awareness? No. It is a movement or appearance within awareness. But can the thought stand apart from awareness? No. It has no independent nature as a thing apart. A thought, as a thought, is only an appearance, but in essence it is only awareness itself.

Keeping all this in mind, you can express the basic understanding of what you are as either 'I am nothing in the appearance' or 'Everything in the appearance is what I am'. Ultimately, what you are is beyond all formulations and statements whatsoever. You are present and aware. That is what you are. It is neither an affirmation nor a negation but an inescapable fact. Seeing this, you give up all attempts to grasp this in the mind and simply rest in and as the one and only thing that is certain and free from doubt—your own being.

100

Clear and Empty, Moment to Moment

Questioner: I am down with a head cold and sinus infection. It is good time to retreat. However, I am still free! There is such a wonderful peace and freedom. I can see I am not the body, although it certainly has been busy taking care of itself.

John: It is nice to hear that everything has come into focus. It is a wonderful discovery to find that everything takes place spontaneously and effortlessly. What needs to be done comes up to be done. Everything goes on as before for the most part, but the burden of being a separate someone running the show drops out of the picture because the concept is seen as false.

Q: Old memories of what to do spring forth for the body, to try different remedies for disease repair.

John: As you can see, there is the natural intelligence of the body and mind to do the needful. It just comes up to do with little fuss or concern. If there is something to be done to bring the situation to balance, you will do it. If not, you still retain a sense of inward composure and peace, knowing that whatever arises does not ultimately touch the essence of what you are.

Q: One urge after another is acted upon spontaneously. There is no choice there! I see that I am not thought, and very little self-centered thought comes up now. If it does, it is questioned. Nothing is sticking.

John: Excellent. With the dropping away of the belief and interest in the thoughts, they just sail through. You can clearly see a self-centered thought for what it is. In that seeing all the fixation just melts away. Without the belief and interest, the thoughts have less and less reason to even arise and you find yourself naturally and effortlessly free of the thoughts and the subsequent chains of emotional bondage and suffering they once generated. The experience is a life free of suffering, doubts, worry and confusion. It is not that those things still go on but you are just detached from them. How and why would self-centered thoughts continue when the central cause is seen as absent? At most, an old habit pattern may arise. After all, those notions and beliefs may have been hanging around for a few years. But you see a thought as a thought, and it sails right through, leaving you clear and empty from moment to moment.

Follow up ...

Q: Okay, we can lay this 'I' thing to rest now. I realized that an other-worldly dropping of the 'I' is not necessary. The 'I' concept, as a concept, still remains. It is what fixes breakfasts, still asks something of another person and pays my credit card bill.

John: As you have seen, the 'I' is just a notion, a thought appearing in awareness. The 'I' is just a word or label used for communication and expression in the appearance. The main thing to see is that you are not that word 'I'. It is a symbol or device with some practical use. That 'I' is just a word that we have been conditioned to apply to the natural and spontaneous functioning of the body and mind. They carry on quite well without that concept.

To be very precise, I would not say that the 'I' is doing anything. How can a lifeless word that bears no relationship to any of the activities be responsible for doing them? Still, as you see, for the purposes of daily communication, there is no harm in saying 'I do this and that'. The main thing is that you see the concept as a concept. In point of fact, the 'I' exists only as a concept. There is no object or appearance that is the actual 'I'. It is a word with no corresponding object. That is why, in the final analysis, there is no such thing as an 'I' at all. There is only the word 'I' and the assumption that that thing is present. Yet when investigated, you find that there is no 'I' at all (except as a word). There is no need for an 'I' to drop away, because there is not any 'I' present that can drop away. What drops away is the belief in the reality of the 'I'. The assumption that such a thing exists is exposed through clear seeing. Because that 'I' is only a belief or an assumption, the investigation exposes and undercuts it.

Q: Now I see this 'I' as a concept only. It arises temporarily in thought as a tool for navigating this play. I know my essence to be the awareness on which this concept appears. That is all that is necessary. Done.

John: The culprit (the 'I' concept') at the center of the production is now clearly exposed for what it is, and your identity as the presence-awareness on which this and all other ideas appear is seen as your essence. Done? I would say well done!

101

The Doubts Are Over

Questioner: I am writing to you after a while, and I am glad to confirm that the search is officially over. The curtains have come down. All the questioning and the separate me, you and others are seen to be—to use the overdone cliché—ultimately waves drifting carelessly over the sea.

I was reading the correspondence of another lady on your website who captured it so beautifully when she said whereas earlier it used to be 'I lost that!' it is now 'Thoughts arise too'. Yes, that is exactly it.

Thoughts are seen as coming and going, much as autumn leaves come and go during fall. Life is akin to a river now—flowing along, meeting some stones and pebbles along the way, but gushing forth all the same. There is no real trouble in anything, not in the computer going bust, not in the Internet freezing (as a freelance writer, I depend on this machine a lot), not in catching a bad cold. They are all part of the flow, and not given the dramatic importance they used to be given earlier. And apparently that seems to 'solve' these 'problems' faster than they even appear. Earlier, these problems would stretch on and on, or more precisely they would be given a lot of juice by the mind.

Life is such a joy now—light, easy, fun-filled. Nothing has changed, none of the outward circumstances or people. Yet everything has changed. This simple, clear awareness lets all be, just the way they are, and hence all seems wondrous and magical. I have found new interests. For example, I have taken to cooking, whereas earlier I loathed even entering the kitchen. I have started taking walks in the morning. My old interests have found a fresh lease of energy and spontaneity that makes pursuing them so much more enjoyable. Worry, anxiety and pessimism have been replaced by naivete, joy and peace. And it is a wellspring that does not finish!

I do not plan to share my insights with others that might 'need' them. I guess if the sharing has to happen, it will, just as spontaneously as everything else does. At the same time, judging apparent others has stopped, for everyone is the same one. It is hard to put in words, but I am sure you understand what I mean.

It has been about a year since I first got pointed to your website. Something was there that kept drawing me back, even though initially I felt your words were a touch dry. I guess I was looking for mystical potions then! Yet, this lack of any mystical frills was precisely what helped me see through the mind's framework in the end. Your pointers, direct and clear, if worked with, can do wonders. It is not the words. It is your relentless conviction coming from the space beyond doubt that does the trick. I can say this now, because I have finally known that space. The doubts are over. The drama is over. The curtains are down. And life is on.

Thanks, John. That is not deifying you. It is just an expression of sincere love and gratitude for showing me the phantom is really harmless, since it is just a phantom.

John: Thank you for being in touch and letting me know how you have been doing since we last communicated. It is always a joy to hear the good news that the simplicity of this has dawned. As you express so well, when the doubts and dramas fall away through seeing what is true about ourselves, we recover a child-like wonder and spontaneity. It was always there, but just got covered over by mistaken thoughts and beliefs that captivated our attention for a time. No harm! Nothing essential is ever lost. With our own sincerity and interest, a few pointers can bring us back to looking for ourselves to see what is true. Now this is your direct experience and no one or no thing can stand in the way of what you know. Whether you share this message with seeming others or not, your life lived in clarity and freedom is its own communication. Words only point, but what is real and true always shines within your heart as the presence of awareness that you can never leave. Thank you for sharing your insights. I enjoyed reading them. Feel free to stay in touch as the spirit moves.

Other titles from Non-Duality Press include:

Nathan Gill

Already Awake

Being: the bottom line

Leo Hartong:

Awakening to the Dream

From Self to Self

John Wheeler

Shining in Plain View

Awakening to the Natural State

'Sailor' Bob Adamson

What's Wrong with Right Now?

Presence-Awareness

John Greven

Oneness

Richard Sylvester

I Hope You Die Soon

Printed in the United States
62997LVS00002B/182